The Hidden Magic of Fairy Tales around the Globe

from a Lightworker's Perspective

Elisabeth Noel

Artwork by Thomas Kay

The first man, who, having fenced in a piece of land, said "This is mine", and found people naive enough to believe him, that man was the true founder of civil society. From how many crimes, wars and murders, from how many horrors and misfortunes might not anyone have saved mankind, by pulling up the stakes and crying to his fellows: Beware of listening to this imposter; you are undone if you once forget that the fruits of the earth belong to us all, and the earth itself to nobody.

Jean-Jacques Rousseau

Discours sur inégalité, 1755
(Discourse on Inequality)

Publisher: © starwater.ie, 2022
Author: © Elisabeth Noel, 2022
Artwork: © Thomas Kay, 2022
Photographs: © Thomas Kay, Marianne Hammer, 2022
Copy editor and proofreader: Thomas Oeschger
Layout: Christine Hirzel
Print: booksfactory.ie

All rights reserved. No part of this publication may be reproduced, stored in a retrieval system, or transmitted in any form or by any means, electronic, mechanical, photocopying, recording or otherwise, for public or private use, other than for "fair use" as brief quotations embodied in articles and reviews, without prior written permission of the appropriate copyright holder.

A catalogue record of this book is available from the British Library

Available as:
Hardcover: ISBN 9781739775001
Paperback: ISBN 9781739775018
E-Book: ISBN 9781739775025

Printed on FSC Paper

Preface		9
A Fairy Cow	Ireland	11
The Flower Queen's Daughter	Bukovina	15
Geirlaug, the King's Daughter	New Iceland	23
The Blue Parrot	France	33
The Death of Koshchei the Deathless	Russia	41
Kupti and Imani	Punjab	51
What Came of Picking Flowers	Portugal	61
The Story of Bensurdatu	Sicily	69
The Story of Prince Ahmed and the Fairy Paribanou	Persia	79
The Magic Kettle	Japan	89
The Enchanted Pig	Rumania	93
The Green Knight	Jutland	103
The Castle of Kerglas	Brittany	111
The Three Wonderful Beggars	Serbia	121
About the artist and his paintings		130
About the author		131

Engraved stone at Fourknocks, Co. Meath, Ireland

Preface

Whenever I find myself in an ancient stone circle here in Ireland or in England, I go from stone to stone and whisper to each one: "Remember, remember! Remember the love, remember the light, remember the sacred dream of creation!"

I remind the stones and myself of a time when the world was ONE, and we all knew that the Divine is within ourselves and not somewhere outside or even above.

Jean-Jaques Rousseau is certainly right if he says that the earth belongs to nobody. If we say and act otherwise, we are woefully ignorant and criminally stupid. My partner and I do own some land on a paper, but we know very well it is not ours to possess, only to guard, to serve, to look after. We plant trees and shrubs and healing plants and flowers. We love the wildlife and feed it in wintertime. We made ponds for the frogs and the toads and many other animals, because in summer our brooks are often dried out. We put up "no shooting" signs. If a storm is approaching, we call on the angels of peace and stillness to be within and around all of us and to protect all living beings. We meditate in our garden and forest and visualize Earth healing. Most of all, we enjoy the incredible beauty of our green and blue planet and communicate with nature beings, with fairies and devas and little dwarfs. We are deeply grateful to be here. A vision I had in our garden led me to the forest of Brocéliande in Brittany. I lived there once a very long time ago as a deva. It was a time when the forests were vast like the oceans and men were few. It was the dreamtime of Earth. I will call this vision: Sacred Space.

I am by the sacred well in the enchanted forest of Brocéliande in Brittany where Merlin met the Fay Viviane. It is springtime. All is quiet and full of light. The air is fresh and pure. The little pond wherein the well springs up is blue as the sky above. Flowers grow around it. Delicate. Almost transparent. Translucent. I am the overlighting Deva of Brocéliande. I sink into the well. Rise up in it. Sparkling with watermagic. My hair streaming out like sunlight. I feel ready to make love. Not to another being but to this beautiful forest. I rise up into the crowns of the ancient trees and further up into the clouds. I float down like a mist, like golden dew. Down into the roots of the trees and into the heart of the Earth. Then I kiss the wellwater and bless it and all the animals that come and drink from it. A stag at first. The king and the soul of the forest. A little hare sits in my lap and a fox draws near, but he does not harm the hare, because we are all one in love and light.

A Fairy Cow

Ireland

There was a story told, twas common knowledge in this area when I was going to school, about this cow, a fairy cow. She used to billet above where the bush is in Latoon, and she used to come down every morning via Clonmoney. And of course, the people o' the parish used to all milk her on the way down. She supplied milk to the poor people of the parish. She was something on the same principle as the manna in the desert. She was a white cow. And you could milk her a million times, and she'd still supply milk.

I inquired of a man that knew the story from his elders. I always heard it when I was going to school, but in order to back up my belief, I asked him. And he told me that some smart aleck on the way bet his neighbour he'd find an utensil that she would not fill. So he produced a sieve and milked her into that. She couldn't fill that of course.

When the facility was abused, she came along until she came to Clonmoney, below the Hurlers Cross. There's a stream crossing the road there called the Sruthan. (Irish for "stream"). She took a drink out o' that stream and she showed up no more. If the Good People (Fairies) take from us what they need when they need it, they can also be generous and helpful neighbours, as in this case, where one of their cattle is sent to help poor people.

Yet how depressingly predictable that human nature so often seems to find a way to abuse kindness to the ultimate loss of everyone.

This story is told in various versions not just all over Ireland (in Irish the cow is known as the Glas Ghoibhneach), but also in Scotland, Wales and parts of England.

Here we have the origin of Fairy Tales: simply stories about the good people, the little people, the friends, the Faerie. I quite agree that in the very beginning we lived together with the fair folk, the lordly ones, the shining ones!

...we walked and played together, for that was the morning of the world... (Marion Zimmer Bradley: Lady of Avalon)
As you probably noticed, dear reader, this is a story directly from an oral source. In Ireland we still have

11

fairy trees and fairy forts and fairy cottages, and we used to have fairy horses, fairy cows and lots and lots of other fairy creatures. When I first came to live here about thirty years ago, I had a fairy dog, Holly, with a delicate snout like a blush pink rose. In my wild garden still stand not only one but two fairy cottages, and the water we drink comes out of a fairy hill.

That this beautiful story is told in so many places in Ireland, England, Wales and Scotland means among other things that long ago it was possible to have a cow in a pasture without anyone driving her away or claiming ownership of her. That alone is quite wonderful. Like the ancient stone circles we need to remember a time when the Earth, her precious animal children and we ourselves were free. We need to remember the sacred dream of creation. Only a few hundred years ago it was still the custom in many a village to give a piece of land to Robin, to the green power, to the nature spirits. And even today, if you want your garden to thrive, it is a very good idea to consecrate a part of it to the fairies and to leave this part completely alone and never enter it.

In J.R.R. Tolkien's "Silmarillion" the main theme is the creation and the history of the silmarils, three great jewels made by one of the Eldar, the elvish people of the stars that did dwell in Valinor, the Blessed Realm. The inner fire of the silmarils was made of the blended light of the two trees of Valinor, Telperion and Laurelin, that were as radiant as the Moon and the Sun. The slilmarils shone like the stars of Varda, they rejoiced in light and received it and gave it back in hues more marvellous than before.

Our deep memory is exactly like the silmarils: it contains everything that is, was and will be. It contains light and love eternal, creation as it was meant to be.

Marion Zimmer Bradley's book "Lady of Avalon" recalls some very beautiful experiences of the deep and far memory. When Caillean, the very first Lady of Avalon, removed the sacred isle from the world with the help of the Queen of Faerie, she was given a golden tablet inscribed with strange characters and "at the sight of them far memory awakened and Caillean knew that they had been written by the men who came from the mighty lands that now lie drowned beneath the sea. And when she touched it, though she had never heard that language with her mortal ears, she knew what words she must say."

Another such incident happens when the Lady and High Priestess of Avalon, Dierna, meets for the first time a girl who wishes to join her sisterhood. A part of her mind sees a tall and slender girl with dark hair. "But there was another feeling which she could only characterize as recognition. Dierna's heart bounded; she blinked, for a moment seeing the girl fragile, with fine pale hair and robed as a priestess, and then again small, with auburn highlights in her dark curls, and golden bracelets curling like serpents around her arms. Who is she, she asked herself, and then, or who

WAS she, and who was I, that I greet her return with such anguished joy?"

The third example is a vision quest on the hill and within the stone circle of Avalon. "The moon was sailing halfway up the heavens; the shadows of the ringstones stretched sharp and black across the circle, but the altar in the centre was fully illuminated, and the silver vessel of water upon it shone as if lit from within. She looked down at the bowl with the unfocused gaze of vision and saw an island lapped by silver seas. Dierna had never seen it with her waking eyes, but she recognized the alternating rings of land and water, the rich fields near the sea and the ships in the inner harbour, and in the center an isle within an island, stepped and terraced and crowned with temples that gleamed pale in the moonlight. Vision expanded; now she gazed upon the island from a terrace with a marble balustrade. A man stood beside her. Tattooed dragons twined the strong forearms that gripped the rail, and the royal diadem of the sun, its disk paled now with moonlight, gleamed on his brow. She knew the spirit that looked out of his eyes. He turned to her and said: Heart of Flame!"

We all have memories like that, some go back very far indeed, some are more recent. It is easy to get hold of terrible things that happened to us, because they are etched very deeply into our memories, but it is more difficult to bring back refined and wonderful images, as they can prove to be quite elusive. No matter how much we train our extrasensory perceptions, we need first of all to know and to trust ourselves. We need to let go of fear and pain and sorrow and anger and to forgive ourselves and those that need our forgiveness. We need to become real and true. So much in our life is a persona, a mask, a pretence. Brainwashing happens as a matter of course in our society, only we are not aware of it, we think this is really what we are or what we should be. I call this rubbish! For the most part we are NOT AT ALL what we think we are.

In truth, we all are what Midir sings in the "Immortal Hour" by Fiona Macleod:

How beautiful they are,
The lordly ones
Who dwell in the hills.
In the hollow hills.

They have faces like flowers,
And their breath is wind
that stirs amid grasses
Filled with white clover.

How beautiful they are,
How beautiful,
The shining ones
In the hollow hills.

The Flower Queen's Daughter

From the Bukowinaer (Bukowina was the crown land of Austria-Hungary from 1867 to 1918)

A young prince was riding one day through a meadow that stretched for miles in front of him, when he came to a deep open ditch. He was turning aside to avoid it, when he heard the sound of someone crying in the ditch. He dismounted from his horse and stepped along in the direction the sound came from. To his astonishment he found an old woman, who begged him to help her out of the ditch. The Prince bent down and lifted her out of her living grave, asking her at the same time how she had managed to get there.

"My son", answered the old woman, "I am a very poor woman, and soon after midnight I set out for the neighbouring town in order to sell my eggs in the market on the following morning; but I lost my way in the dark and fell into this deep ditch, where I might have remained for ever but for your kindness."

Then the prince said to her: "You can hardly walk; I will put you on my horse and lead you home. Where do you live?"

"Over there, at the edge of the forest in the little hut you see in the distance", replied the old woman.

The prince lifted her on to his horse, and soon they reached the hut, where the old woman got down, and turning to the prince said: "Just wait a moment and I will give you something." And she disappeared into her hut, but returned very soon and said: "You are a mighty prince, but at the same time you have a kind heart, which deserves to be rewarded. Would you like to have the most beautiful woman in the world to be your wife?"

"Most certainly I would!" replied the prince.

So the old woman continued: "The most beautiful woman in the whole world is the daughter of the Queen of Flowers, who has been captured by a dragon. If you wish to marry her, you must first set her free, and this I will help you to do. I will give you this little bell. If you ring it once, the King of the Eagles will appear; if you ring it twice, the King of Foxes will come to you; and if you ring it three times, you will see the King of the Fishes by your side. These will aid you if you are in difficulty. Now farewell, and heaven prosper your undertaking." She handed him the little bell, and there disappeared hut and all, as though the earth had swallowed her up.

Then it dawned on the prince that he had been speaking to a good fairy, and putting the little bell carefully in his pocket, he rode home and told his father that he meant to set the daughter of the Flower Queen free, and intended setting out on the following day into the wide world in search of the maid.

So the next morning the prince left his home. He had roamed round the world for a whole year, and suffered much from want and misery, but still he had come on no trace of her he was in search of. At last one day he came to a hut, in front of which sat a very old man. The prince asked him: "Do you know where the dragon lives who keeps the daughter of the Flower Queen prisoner?"

"No, I do not", answered the old man. "But if you go straight along this road for a year, you will reach a hut, where my father lives, and possibly he may be able to tell you."

The prince thanked him for his information and continued his journey for a whole year along the same road, and at the end of it came to a little hut, where he found a very old man. He asked him the same question, and the old man said: "No, I do not know where the Dragon lives. But go straight along this road for another year, and you will come to a hut, in which my father lives. I know he can tell you!"

And so the prince wandered on for another year, always on the same road, and at last reached the hut where he found the third old man. He put the same question to him as he had put to his son and grandson; but this time the old man answered: "The dragon lives up there on the mountain, and he has just began his year of sleep. For one whole year he is always awake, and the next he sleeps. But if you wish to see the Flower Queen's daughter go up the second mountain. The dragon's old mother lives there, she has a ball every night, to which the Flower Queen's daughter goes regularly."

So the prince went up the second mountain, where he found a castle all made of gold with diamond windows. He opened the big gate leading into the courtyard, and was just going to walk in, when seven dragons rushed on him and asked him what he wanted.

The prince replied: "I have heard so much of the beauty and kindness of the dragon's mother, and would like to enter her service." This flattering speech pleased the dragons, and the eldest of them said: "You may come with me, and I will take you to the mother dragon."

They entered the castle and walked through twelve splendid halls, all made of gold and diamonds. In the twelfth room they found the mother dragon seated on a diamond throne. She was the ugliest woman under the sun, and, added to it all, she had three heads. Her appearance was a great shock to the prince, and so was her voice, which was like the croaking of many ravens. She asked him: "Why have you come here?"

The prince answered at once: "I have heard so much of your beauty and kindness that I would very much like to enter your service." – "Very well", said the mother dragon: "But if you wish to serve me, you must first lead my mare out to the meadow and look after her for three days; but if you don't bring her home safely every evening, we will eat you up."

The prince undertook the task and led the mare out to the meadow. But no sooner had they reached the grass than she vanished. The prince sought for her in vain, and at last in despair sat down on a big stone and contemplated his sad fate. As he sat thus lost in thought, he noticed an eagle flying over his head. Then he suddenly bethought him of his little bell, and taking it out of his pocket he rang it once. In a moment he heard a rustling sound in the air beside him, and the King of the Eagles sank at his feet.

"I know what you want of me", he said. "You are looking for the mother dragon's mare who is galloping about among the clouds. I will summon all the eagles of the air together, and order them to catch the mare and bring her to you." And with these words the King of the Eagles flew away. Towards evening the prince heard a mighty rushing sound in the air, and when he looked up he saw the eagles driving the mare before them. They sank to the ground and gave the mare over to him. Then the prince rode home to the old mother dragon, who was full of wonder when she saw him, and said: "You have succeeded today in looking after my mare, and as a reward you shall come to my ball tonight." She gave him a cloak made of copper, and led him to a big room where several dragons were dancing. Here too was the Flower Queen's beautiful daughter. Her dress was woven out of the most lovely flowers in the world, and her complexion was like lilies and roses. As the prince was dancing with her, he managed to whisper in her ear: "I have come to set you free!"

Then the beautiful girl said to him: "If you succeed in bringing the mare back safely the third day, ask the Mother Dragon to give you a foal of the mare as a reward."

The ball came to an end at midnight, and early next morning the Prince again led the mother dragon's mare out into the meadow. But again she vanished before his eyes. Then he took out his little bell and rang it twice. In a moment the King of the Foxes stood before him and said: "I know already what you want, and will summon all the foxes together to find the mare who has hidden herself in a hill." With these words the King of Foxes disappeared, and in the evening the foxes brought the mare to the prince.

Then he rode home to the mother dragon, from whom he received this time a cloak made of silver, and again she invited him to the ball. The Flower Queen's daughter was delighted to see him safe and sound, and when they were dancing together she whispered in his ear: "If you succeed again tomorrow, wait for me with the foal in the meadow. After the ball we will fly away together."

On the third day the prince led the mare to the meadow again, and once more she vanished before his eyes. The prince took out his little bell and rang it three times. The King of Fishes appeared: "I know quite well what you want me to do, and I will summon the fishes of the sea together and tell them to bring the mare to you." Towards evening the mare was returned to him, and when he led her home to the mother dragon, she said: "You are a brave youth, and I will make you my body-servant. What shall I give you as a reward?" The prince begged for a foal of the mare, which the mother dragon gave him, and over and above, a cloak made of gold, because he had praised her beauty.

So in the evening he appeared at the ball in his golden cloak; but before the entertainment was over he slipped *away and went straight to the stables, where he mounted his foal and rode out into the meadow to wait for the Flower Queen's daughter. Towards midnight the beautiful girl appeared, and placing her in front of him on his horse, the prince and she flew like the wind till they reached the Flower Queen's dwelling. But the dragons had noticed their flight, and woke their brother out of his year's sleep. He flew into a terrible rage when he heard what had happened, and determined to lay siege to the Flower Queen's palace. But the Queen caused a forest of magic flowers as high as the sky to grow up round her dwelling, through which no-one could force a way.*

The Flower Queen said to the prince: "I will give my consent to your marriage with my daughter gladly, but she can only stay with you in summer. In winter when the earth is covered with snow, she must come and live with me." The prince agreed and led his beautiful bride home, where the wedding was celebrated with great magnificence.

At first the prince has no idea that the old woman he helps out of a ditch and gives a ride to on his horse is a fairy. Believe me, we VERY often do not know that we have an encounter with a fairy. And unless we hold an intent for the highest good for all creation AND act on this intent the best way we can, thus becoming one with the fair folk, we may never know. The young prince could have ignored the old woman in the ditch or later let her find her own way home. If so, he would never have recognized her her as a mighty spiritual power. We can pass through life blind as bats, except that bats are anything but. But that's just another of our many errors concerning the animal kingdom.

If you, dear reader, would tell your parents (who expect you to do well in your studies or to go and look for a job and when you have found one stick to it) that you rather wanted to set the daughter of the Flower Queen free and intended to go out into the wide world to search for her tomorrow morning, your parents would most likely take you to a psychiatrist, and the latter would typically have no understanding of your wishes either. Therefore you would probably be heavily sedated until you forgot all about faries and dragons and Flower Queens. This is more or less what happened to a young lass here in Ireland who had seen angels all her life and talked to them. She was shut away and later she was under orders to see a psychiatrist every week and take the pills he gave her.

Fortunately she married a nice guy who backed her up when she decided to throw the pills into the loo. Later her husband and her children were truly delighted to have a wife and a mother who was clairvoyant and clairaudient. Good for them!

The first old man in our fairy tale can give the prince the glad tidings that he has chosen the right way. But he needs to continue on this path for a long time and go back into the past to the old man's father, and even further back to his grandfather to get the information he needs.

When I came to Ireland many years ago to live in an old farmhouse, I too, like the prince, suffered from want and misery. I was poor, and often I did not have enough firewood to keep the draughty and damp old house warm. But it was the right way of life for me. After some years I too started to find what I was looking for, but it was a long time until I got a clearer idea what was expected of me as a lightworker.

Of course I am still searching. I got and I get a lot of help from my fairy allies and my power animals and from the angels and nature spirits around me, from trees and from the elements. I have learned to listen to all of them and to the men and women that hold the earth wisdom and the wisdom of the stars above us. One of my closest friends is a mighty dragon in all the colours of fire and of forests, red, orange, gold and many different hues of green. I once brought light into the dark world where he lived, and the light made it very beautiful. Later, when the dragon came with me into the upper world to bring some lost souls into its splendour, the dragon received a golden sun diadem from a radiant sun being. Now he wears it proudly and happily when we travel together.

In fairy tales dragons can be good or evil. They can hold a maid prisoner or they can guard her, or even both. The Flower Queen's daughter does not exactly lead the life of your ordinary prisoner, dancing every night in a castle made of gold and diamonds.

Black magicians can conjure up dark dragons that have their life force from blood sacrifice. These are no real dragons, but terrible illusions that can cause much harm. True dragons are cosmic guardians and full of wisdom. They hold the key to the knowledge of all knowledge, the secrets of white magic.

There is a German fairy tale "Das Rosenmädchen" (The Rose Maiden) that is much alike to "The Flower Queen's Daughter." It is often said that the rose is the Queen of Flowers, so her daughter would therefore be the rose maiden or the rose princess. In the German version it is not a fairy that gives the magic bell to the hero, it is his mother, the forest-woman. The rose maiden is also guarded by a dragon, and the hero is given the same task of looking after the mare of the dragon's mother with the very same results.

The dragon who lives on a mountain and sometimes sleeps a long time reminds us of a volcano. Like the dragon, the volcano can sleep for years and then awake and belch forth fire.

In a great many fairytales we encounter animals that relate to the four elements. Here we have the King of Eagles to represent air, the King of Foxes to represent earth, the King of Fishes to represent water, and the dragon (volcano) is obviously the spirit of fire. But it is usually only after the prince showed compassion to animals that they consent to aid him in his quest. In our fairytale the prince did already prove his worth by helping the old lady out of the ditch.

The language of fairytales is universal in the true sense of the word. It is indeed the universe that talks to us through wonderful and magic stories and in every tongue known. We are told again and again to help one another and to love and respect all living beings. We are told that things are often not what they appear to be, and that it is perfectly okay to follow our heart's desire and make our dreams come true, no matter how crazy those dreams may seem. We hear that nothing and no-one is more powerful than animals, and that the world is wonderous beyond everything we ever thought possible.

That appearances can be a tricky business we realize when we read the description of the mother of dragons. She is said to be the ugliest woman under the sun. Care to have another look at her? Christine Arana Fader writes in her little handbook of dragons ("Das kleine Drachen Handbuch") about the mother of dragons:

"Wenn du der Drachenkönigin Alba entgegentrittst, wirst du für einen Moment geblendet von ihrem Licht. Sie ist erhaben und wunderschön, sie steht für Freiheit und Liebe. Ihr Licht vermischt sich mit den zarten Klängen ihrer Aura und verströmt eine geheimnisvolle, einzigartige Schwingung, die sich im ganzen Raum der Galaxie verbreitet."

(If you meet the queen of dragons, her light will almost blind you. She is serene and marvellously beautiful. Her light blends with the music of her aura and sends out a unique vibration that can be felt in the entire galaxy.)

What does the mother of dragons want with the rose maiden, the daughter of the Queen of Flowers? In the secrets of the tarot, the rose is the princess of the kingdom of Earth, a mighty power, in many ways even more powerful than the Earth Queen herself. She is a virgin, in the ancient meaning of this word, a woman on her own, not dependent on a man. If we see the mother of dragons as a guardian to the rose maiden, she certainly seems to make sure that only a worthy man can get hold of her, one that showed compassion to the old woman in the ditch and earned the magic bell. One that has the courage to face the mother of dragons in her most hideous aspect. One that can talk to the elements like Christ did when he soothed the storm on the lake Genezareth.

The prince and the daughter of the Flower Queen waste no time with declarations of love. They focus at once on the main point: Freedom! Life is not worth living without freedom, it is not even real life, only a rather futile exercise in survival and endurance.

It is high time for every human being to make freedom and truth an absolute priority. Of course freedom is first and last a spiritual capacity. A slave is likely to be far more free than his master.

The foal of the mother dragons mare, who carries the prince with his bride to the Flower Queen like the wind, is indeed the great power of the air, the storm. That the daughter of the Flower Queen can only live with the prince in summer is the exact opposite to the daughter of the Greek goddess Demeter, Persephone, who lived with her dark bridegroom in his palace of death beneath the earth in winter and returned every spring to her mother. Here the rose princess can spend the golden days of summer with her beloved.

The Queen of Flowers reminds me of William Butler Yeats' poem "Secret Rose":

…"far-off, most secret and inviolet Rose Enfold me in my hour of hours"…

The prince is like

…"him who sold tillage and house and goods,
And sought through lands and islands numberless years,
Until he found, with laughter and with tears,
A woman of so shining loveliness
that men threshed corn at midnight by a tress,
a little stolen tress"…

Both the mother of dragons and the Queen of Flowers are synonyms for the goddess. They both protect what they value most, namely the Shekina, the perfect rose, the female soul of creation and its ultimate mystery.

Geirlaug, the King's Daughter

New Iceland, Canada

One day, a powerful king and his beautiful wife were sitting in the gardens of the capital city, talking earnestly about the future life of their little son, who was sleeping by their side in his beautiful golden cradle. They had been married for many years without children, so when this baby came they thought themselves the happiest couple in the whole world. He was a fine sturdy little boy, who loved to kick and to strike out with his fists; but even if he had been weak and small, they would still have thought him the most wonderful creature upon earth, and so absorbed were they in making plans for him, that they never noticed a huge dark shadow creeping up, till a horrible head with gleaming teeth stretched over them, and in an instant their beloved baby was snatched away.

For a while the king and queen remained where they were, frozen with horror. Then the king rose slowly, and holding out his hand to his wife, led her weeping into the palace, and for many days their subjects saw no more of them.

Meanwhile, the dragon soared high into the air, holding the cradle between his teeth, and the baby still slept on. He flew so fast that he soon crossed the borders of another kingdom, and again he beheld the king and queen of the country seated in the garden with a little girl lying in a cradle of white satin and lace. Swooping down from behind as he had done before, he was just about to seize the cradle, when the king jumped up and dealt him such a blow with his golden staff that the dragon not only started back but, in his pain, let fall the boy, as he spread his wings and soared into the air away from all danger.

"That was a narrow escape", said the king, turning to his wife, who sat pale with fright, and clasping her baby tightly in her arms. "Horrible", murmured the queen, "but look, what is that glittering object that is lying out there?" The king walked in the direction of her finger, and to his astonishment beheld another cradle and another baby.

"Ah, the monster must have stolen this as he sought to steal Geirlaug", cried he. And stooping lower, he read some words that were written on the fine linen that was wound round the boy. "This is Grethari, son of Grethari, the king!" Unfortunately, it happened that the two neighbouring monarchs had had a serious quarrel and for some years had ceased holding communication with each other. So, instead of sending a messenger at once to Grethari to tell him of the safety of his son, the king contented himself with adopting the baby-boy, and he was brought up with Geirlaug, the princess.

For a while things went well with the children, who were as happy as the day was long, but at last there came a time when the queen could no more run races or play hide-and-seek with them in the garden as she was fond of doing, but lay and watched them from a pile of soft cushions. By-and-by she gave up doing even that, and people in the palace spoke with low voices, and even Geirlaug and Grethari trod gently and moved quietly when they drew near her room. At length, one morning, they were sent for by the king himself, who, his eyes red with weeping, told them that the queen was dead.

Great was the sorrow of the two children, for they had loved the queen very dearly, and life seemed dull without her. But the lady-in-waiting who took care of them in the tower which had been built for them while they were still babies, was kind and good, and when the king was busy or away in other parts of his kingdom she made them quite happy, and saw that they were taught everything that a prince and princess ought to know. Two or three years passed, when, one day, as the children were anxiously awaiting their father's return from a distant city, there rode post haste into the courtyard of the palace a herald whom the king had sent before him, to announce that he was bringing back a new wife.

Now, in itself, there was nothing very strange or dreadful in the fact that the king should marry again, but, as the lady-in-waiting soon guessed, the queen, in spite of her beauty, was an evil witch, and as it was easy to see that she was jealous of everyone who might gain power over her husband, it boded ill for Geirlaug and Grethari. The faithful woman could not sleep for thinking about her charges, and her heart sank when, a few months after the marriage, war broke out with a country across the sea, and the king rode away at the head of his troops. Then, one night, the witch came to the tower, and when the sun rose, the beds of Grethari and Geirlaug were empty. At dawn the queen summoned some of her guards and told them that she had been warned in a dream of some danger through a wild beast, and bade them go out and kill every animal within two miles of the palace. But the only beast they found were two black foals of wonderous beauty. It seemed a pity to kill them, for what harm could two little foals do anyone? So they let them run away, frisking over the plain, and returned to the palace.

"Did you see nothing, really nothing?" asked the queen. "Nothing, your majesty", they replied. But the queen did not believe them. She gave orders to her steward that at supper the guards should be plied with strong drink, and further, he was to report to her whatever they might let fall. Late in the evening the steward told the queen: "I listened to their talk from beginning to end, and nothing did they see save two black foals." The look in the queens blazing eyes terrified him, and, bowing hastily, he backed quickly out of her presence.

In a weeks time the king came home, and right glad were all the courtiers to see him. "Now perhaps she will find someone else to scream at", they said, for the queen had vented her rage on her attendants these days, though what had happened to make her so angry nobody knew. But whatever might be the meaning of it, things would be sure to improve with the king to rule in the palace instead of his wife. But the very first morning after the king's arrival the queen related the dream she had dreamed in his absence and begged him to go out and kill every living creature he saw within two miles of the city. The king, who always believed everything the queen said, promised to do as she wished. But before he had ridden through the lovely gardens that surrounded the palace, he was attracted by the singing of two little blue birds perched on a scarlet-berried holly, which made him think of everything beautiful that he had ever heard of or imagined. Hour after hour passed by, and still the birds sang, and still the king listened, though he never guessed that it was Geirlaug and Grethari whose songs filled him with enchantment. At length darkness fell; the birds voices hushed, and the king awoke with a start to find that for that day his promise to the queen could not be kept.

"Well! did you see anything?" she asked eagerly, when the king entered her apartments. "Ah, my dear, I am almost ashamed to confess to you. But the fact is that before I rode as far as the western gate, the singing of two strange blue birds made me forget all else in the world. However, to-morrow nothing shall hinder me from fullfilling your desires."

"There will be no to-morrow", muttered the queen, as she turned away with a curious glitter in her eyes. But the king did not hear her.

That night the king gave a great supper in the palace in honour of the victory he had gained over the enemy. It was easy for the queen to pour a slow but fatal poison in the kings cup. Before dawn the palace was roused by the news that the king was dead. Of course nobody's cries and laments were as loud as those of the queen. But once the funeral was over, she gave out that she was going to shut herself up in a distant castle till the year of her mourning was over. After appointing a regent of the kingdom, she set out attended only by a maid who knew all her secrets. Once she had left the palace, she quickly began to work her spells, to discover under what form Geirlaug and Grethari lay hidden. Luckily, the princess had studied magic under a wise woman, so she was able to fathom her stepmother's wicked plot, and hastily changed herself into a whale, and her foster-brother into its fin. But the queen took the shape of a shark and gave chase.

For several hours a fierce battle raged between the whale and the shark, and the sea around them was red with blood. Finally it became plain that the victory was to the whale. But when the shark floated dead on the surface of the water, the whale was so exhausted that she had only strength enough to drag her wounded body into a quiet little bay. For three days she remained there as still and motionless as if she had been dead herself. At length her wounds were healed, and she began to think what it was best to do.

"Let us go to your father's kingdom", she said to Grethari when they had both resumed their human shapes and were sitting on a cliff above the sea. "How clever you are! I never thought of that!" answered Grethari, who, in truth, was not clever at all. Geirlaug took a small box of white powder from her dress and sprinkled some over him and some over herself, and, quicker than lightning, they found themselves in the palace garden from which Grethari had been carried off so many years ago.

"Now take the band with the golden letters and bind it about your fore-head", said Geirlaug, "and go boldly up to the castle. And remember, however great may be your thirst, you must drink nothing till you have first spoken to your father. If you do, ill will befall us both."

"Why should I be thirsty?" replied Grethari, staring at her in astonishment. "It will not be five minutes to reach the castle gate." Geirlaug held her peace, but her eyes had in them a sad look. "Good-bye", she said at last and kissed him.

Grethari did not reach the castle in five minutes. To his surprise, the door which stood wide open never appeared to come any nearer. The sun burned, and his tongue was parched with thirst. "I don't understand! What can be the matter with me?" he murmured to himself as his knees began to knock under him with fatigue, and his head to swim. He staggered on blindly, when, suddenly, the sound of rushing water came to his ears. In a little wood that bordered the path he beheld a stream falling over a rock. At this sight his promise to Geirlaug was forgotten. Fighting his way through the brambles that tore his clothes, he cast himself down beside the fountain and drank.

When he rose up, his remembrance of Geirlaug and of his past life had vanished. He beheld a white-haired man and woman who stood in the open door with outstretched hands. "Grethari! So you have come home at last!" cried they.

For a long time Geirlaug waited for Grethari, and then she began to understand what had happened. Her heart was heavy, but she soon made up her mind what to do. She left the royal gardens and found a small house where the forester lived with his two daughters.

"Do you want a girl to sweep and to milk the cows?" she asked, when one of the sisters answered her knock. "Yes, we do, very badly; and as you look strong and clean, we will take you for a servant." replied the young woman. "What is your name?" – "Laupherta", said Geirlaug, for she did not wish anyone to know who she was, and following her new mistress into the house, she begged to be taught her work without delay. And so clever was she that, by-and-by, it began to be noised abroad that the strange girl who had come to live in the forester's house had not her equal in the whole kingdom for skill as well as beauty. Thus years slipped away. One day, when she was gathering herbs, Grethari came upon her.

"What is your name, pretty maiden?"
"Laupherta", answered the girl, with a low curtsy.

"Ah! It is you then, of whom I have heard so much", said he. "You are too beautiful to spend your life serving the foresters daughters. Come with me to the palace, and my mother, the queen, will make you one of her ladies in waiting." – "Truly, that would be a great fortune", replied the maiden. "And if you really mean it, I will go with you. But how shall I know that you are not jesting?"

"Give me something to do for you, and I will do it, whatever it is", cried the young man eagerly. And she cast down her eyes and answered: "Go to the stable, and bind the calf that is there so that it shall not break loose in the night and wander away, for the forester and his daughters have treated me well, and I would not leave them with aught of my work still undone."

So Grethari set out for the stable where the calf stood, and tried to bind it, but he found that a coil of the rope had twisted itself round his wrist, and pull as he might, he could not get free. All night he wriggled and struggled in vain. But when the sun rose, the rope suddenly fell away from him, and, very angry with the maiden, he dragged himself back to the palace, flung himself on his bed and slept all day.

Not long after this adventure, the king and queen sent their beloved son to a neighbouring country to seek a bride from among seven princesses. He chose one, and the young pair took ship without delay for the kingdom of the prince's parents. The wind was fair and the vessel swift, and soon the harbour nearest the castle was reached. A splendid carriage had been left there, but no horses were to be found, for every one had been carried off to take part in a great review which the king was to hold that day in honour of his son's marriage.

"I can't stay here all day", said the princess crossly, when Grethari told her of the plight they were in. "You will have to find something to draw the carriage. If you don't, I will sail straight back to my father." Grethari hastily bade his attendants to go in search of some animal. At length a girl appeared driving a young ox in front of her. "Will you lend me your ox, fair maiden?" asked Grethari. "You shall fix your own price, and it shall be paid ungrudgingly."

"My price is seats for me and my two friends behind you and your bride at the wedding feast", answered she. To this Grethari joyfully consented.

Six horses would not have drawn the coach at the speed of this one ox. Trees and fields flew by so fast that the bride became quite giddy. They drew up at the door of the palace in no time. Everything was ready for the marriage, and the oldest men and women in the town agreed that nothing so splendid had ever been seen as the bridal procession to the great hall where the banquet was to be held, before the ceremony was celebrated in the palace. The princess was in high good humour, and taking the prince's hand, she sailed proudly down the room, where the guests were already assembled, to her place at the head of the table by the side of the bridegroom. As she did so, three strange ladies in shining dresses of blue, green and red glided in and seated themselves immediately behind the young couple. The red lady was Geirlaug, who had brought with her the forester's daughters. In one hand she held a wand of birch bark, and in the other a closed basket.

Silently they sat as the feast proceeded; hardly anyone noticed their presence. Suddenly, when the merriment was at its height, Geirlaug opened the basket, and out flew a cock and a hen. To the astonishment of everyone, the birds circled about in front of the royal pair, the cock plucking the feathers out of the tail of the hen, who tried in vain to escape from him.

"Will you treat me as badly as Grethari treated Geirlaug?" cried the hen at last. And Grethari started up wildly. In an instant all the past rushed back to him; the princess by his side was forgotten, and he only saw the face of the girl with whom he had played long years ago.

"Where is Geirlaug?" he exclaimed, looking around the hall; and his eyes fell upon the strange lady. With a smile she held out a ring which he had given her on her twelfth birthday. "You and none other shall be my wife", he said, taking her hand.

It is not easy to describe the scene that followed. Nobody understood what was happening, and the king and the queen imagined that their son had suddenly gone mad. As for the princess, her rage and fury were beyond belief. The guests left the hall as quickly as they could, so the royal family might arrange their own affair. In the end it was settled that half the kingdom must be given to the despised princess, instead of a husband. She sailed back at once to her country, where she was soon betrothed to a young noble, whom she liked much better than Grethari.

That evening Grethari was married to Geirlaug, and they lived happily and made all their people happy also.

A king and his queen are "the happiest couple in the whole world". The cause of this happiness is their son, "the most wonderful creature on earth". They make plans for him without in the least considering what he might one day wish for himself. Obviously, they are in a precarious situation. This kind of good luck is incredibly fragile. The monster that is creeping up like a huge dark shadow, is fear.

Fear is not our natural state of mind. And neither is it natural for anyone to be more fortunate than the rest of mankind. Happiness is meant for All that Is, and we all know that quite well. The moment we assume that we should have more than others, more power, more wealth, more land, more pleasure, we create fear. And the longer we elevate ourselves above others by whatever means, the more we feed this fear, until it has a life of its own. And then: goodbye happiness.

The second king knows how to deal with fear that swoops suddenly down from behind. The golden staff in his hand can be anything that is stronger than fear. Christ said that love can drive out all our worries and anxieties, and this is perfectly true. It is a great pity our fairytale makes fear appear in the form of a dragon, because, as I already mentioned, real dragons are wise and wonderful and guardians of cosmic knowledge, as anyone knows who has studied white magic.

That two neighbouring monarchs have a serious quarrel is not unusual. The thirty year war, the hundred year war, the first and the second world war and many other large-scale hostile manoeuvres of mankind make that abundantly clear. To abduct the heir to a throne is quite in keeping with this state of affairs, but it is nevertheless a crime that has to be paid for sooner or later. Here the price is the life of the queen. She is the one who might have influenced the king to restore the child to his rightful parents, she is in a way his conscience, and now, after a long illness, his conscience is dead.

When we have left the path of truth and honesty, we often stray farther and farther away from all that could be helpful to us. The king marries an evil witch and his children are transformed into black horses. The witch does not kill Geirlaug and Grethari, she gives orders for others to do her dirty work for her. Black magicians have no real power, that is why they are so jealous of those who have it. They have not even courage. All they can do really well is lie. But in this one thing they excel: They can make anyone doubtful and confused. Why is the king not aware that his children are missing? Because the queen has him under her spell. Because his mind is disturbed. He runs out of the palace to do her bidding and kill every living creature within two miles of the city. We are forcibly reminded of Hitlers "Endlösung". Only a king gone mad could promise to follow such an order. However, very often when a new house is being built, I have noticed that all the plants around the building site are ruthlessly wiped out. With the trees and the bushes and the flowers depart the birds and the butterflies and the rest of the modest wildlife that is still amongst the living. Mad, totally mad. When my partner and myself planned to build our new, round, green house, we first tended the land around it. We planted trees, bushes, healing plants and wild flowers. Then I made a little round spirit house and placed it beneath a fairy tree. So, when our new, round, green house finally went up, some of the trees we had planted were already almost fully grown.

White magic serves the light and creates life, black magic denies the light and acts against life. The word "evil" is "live" pronounced backwards. Death.

The king dies of a slow working poison. Nothing is more deadly than lies. It has indeed the effect of a slow working poison in our system. As soon as the king is gone, the queen does her utmost to annihilate his children. But now, Geirlaug, the king's daughter, reveals her true self. The first shapeshifting of the royal children into black foals is an act of black magic. But the blue birds, who sing so sweetly that the king is reminded of everything good and true and beautiful that he ever heard of or imagined, this is clearly the work of a powerful white magician. Geirlaug has been taught by a wise woman, and she learned her lessons well. She has come into her own.

In ancient times the king ruled often through his wife. She was the source of his power. We still see signs of this in some of our myths and fairytales. For instance the mighty queen Leda in Greece, whose consort was Zeus, gave birth to Klytämnestra and the beautiful Helena. Helena left her husband and went to Troy where women still held full power and the queen of the amazons, Penthesilea, was an ally to Hekuba, the queen of Troy. Klytämnestra killed her husband, who had slaughtered her daughter Iphigeneia, and ruled supreme.

In Shakespeare's drama "Hamlet" the grown-up son of the queen is not on the throne. His uncle is king simply because he married the queen.

The famous tale of King Arthur, that has been re-written many times by eager monks, was originally a very different story. Ghwenhwywar brings the round table to Camelot. The idea of democracy. She chooses Lancelot as her knight and lover. She is identical with the fairy queen and also with the white goddess. The mother of Arthur, Igraine, is a daughter of the holy island, Avalon, and of a high priestess thereof. She gives wisdom and authority to rule the land first to Gorlois and later to Uther Pendragon. Her daughter Morgana is one of the last of the wise and magic women of Avalon that we know of. She took her dying brother Arthur to the holy island. She became once again the guardian of the sword Excalibur. She protected the secret of the holy grail. She was without a doubt a very great lady.

Maria, the mother of Christ, was an initiated priestess, as was her daughter in law, Maria Magdalena. Hers is another story that was re-written often by clever males to suit their patriarchal claims and ambitions.

In the story of Geirlaug, the bridegroom, Grethari, is a blockhead. In many fairytales the simpleton has all the luck. Grethari certainly needs it. He is in such a hurry to forget the girl who saved his life and brought him back to his parents. He also needs to be a prince. He would not last long as a servant to the forester. We can see that when he tries to bind the calf and instead twists the rope around his wrist and sleeps all day afterwards. He is not even able to find a horse to draw his splendid carriage.

In a great many fairytales in a great many countries the bride-groom forgets all about his bride. Siegfried for instance could not remember his love für Brünhilde after Kriemhilde cast her spell over him. But Grethari cannot blame any spell, he simply lacks the willpower to keep his promise and to control his thirst. It is clear that thirst stands here for any human desire. There is nothing wrong with desire. But we must all learn to master it, otherwise it will master us and this leads to addiction. We all know there has never been a genuine artist, let alone a great teacher of mankind, without rigorous discipline. When I studied music and drama as a young woman, I knew I had to give my very best, to be fully present and to work my butt off to get anywhere. But as a lighwork student

I worked even harder. Of course, nowadays the human race is addicted to nearly every blooming thing, to money, to fame, to sex, to television, to computers, to drugs, to alcohol and most of all, to death. One way out of addiction is to give the soul her due. Addiction is mostly compensation for something our soul lacks. In the five years I dedicated to learning lightwork healing my addictions vanished like snow in the sun. All that time music was of vital importance to me to refresh my spirit. Mozart and Bach were my constant companions whenever I had a free moment.

In the reality of myth there is no time as we know it. When Grethari returns to his parents, he could be starting a new life altogether. His time with Geirlaug might very well be a past life, another incarnation. It would be less difficult to understand his memory-loss if it were so.

When we come to this planet we often have a mission, a task we have to carry out. We may also have made a promise to unite with others that share our commitment. Any kind of licentiousness will make it hard for us to remember who we truly are and why we were born on earth. The sad look in the eyes of Geirlaug give us an indication that she knows she cannot count on Gretharis' faith and that she has once again to do all the work for him and herself all alone. Believe me, I have seen this sad look often in a woman's or in a man's eyes. However, it is still very much a man's world we live in, and the labour of women too often goes largly unnoticed and unrewarded. How serious a broken promise is, we can see at the end of the tale when the despised princess takes possession of half a kingdom as she sails back to her parents palace.

Whatever Grethari's difficulties to be true to himself may be, it is obvious that Geirlaug has no problems whatsoever in this direction. She takes on another name for herself and her job has no resemblance to anything she was raised to do as a princess, and yet, she takes to it as a duck takes to water. She knows who she is no matter what circumstances she finds herself in. Her resourcefulness does not even fail her when Grethari becomes engaged to a rather vain and useless female. She literally opens her basket at the wedding feast, and her cock and his hen display marital bliss in front of the royal couple. I honestly can't help wishing Geirlaug might find a man who is a bit more worthy of all the efforts she makes on his behalf. But there you are, true love is unconditional. And as king and queen they do make their people happy, it says. I hope it is true. Half their land and the people with it has been given away. But with the friendship of the forester and his daughters and the knowledge of the wise women, Geirlaug will probably manage, even without much help from her husband.

The Blue Parrot

Le Cabinet des Fées; France

In a part of Arabia where groves of palms and sweet-scented flowers give the traveller rest after toilsome journeys under burning skies, there reigned a young king whose name was Lino. He had grown up under the wise rule of his father, who had lately died, and though he was only nineteen, he did not believe, like many young men, that he must change all the laws in order to show how clever he was, but was content with the old ones, which had made the people happy and the country prosperous. There was only one fault that his subjects had to find with him, and that was that he did not seem in any hurry to be married.

The neighbouring kingdom was governed by the Swan fairy, who had an only daughter, the princess Hermosa, who was as charming in her way as Lino in his. The Swan fairy always had an ambassador at the young king's court, and on hearing the grumbles of the citizens that Lino showed no signs of taking a wife, the good man resolved that he would try his hand at matchmaking. "For", he said, "if there is anyone living who is worthy of the princess Hermosa, he is to be found here."

Now, of course it was not proper to offer the princess in marriage, but the ambassador was well used to the ways of the court, and after several conversations on the art of painting, which Lino loved, he led the talk to portraits, and mentioned that a particularly fine picture had lately been made of his own princess.
"Though as for likeness", he concluded, "perhaps it is hardly as good as this small miniature, which was painted a year ago."

The king took it and looked at it closely. "Ah", he sighed, "that must be flattered! It cannot be possible that any woman should be such a miracle of beauty."

"If you could only see her", answered the ambassador.

The king did not reply, but the ambassador was not at all surprised when, the following morning, he was sent for and led into the royal presence.

"Since you showed me that picture", began Lino, almost before the door was shut, "I have not been able to banish the face of the princess from my thoughts. I have summoned you here to inform you that I am about to send special envoys to the court of the Swan fairy, asking for her daughter in marriage."

"I cannot, as you will understand, speak for my mistress in so important a matter", replied the ambassador, "but I know that she will be highly gratified at your proposal."

"If that is so", cried the king, his whole face beaming with joy, "then instead of sending envoys, I will go myself and take you with me. In three days my preparations will be made, and we will set out."

Unluckily for Lino, his neighbour on the other side of the kingdom was a powerful magician named Ismenor, who was king of the Isle of Lions, and the father of a hideous daughter, whom he thought the most beautiful creature that ever existed. Riquette was her name, and she had also fallen in love with a portrait, but it was of king Lino, and she implored her father to give him to her for a husband. Ismenor, who considered that no man living was worthy of his treasure, was about to send his chief minister to king Lino on this mission, when the news reached him that the king had already started for the court of the Swan fairy. Riquette was thrown into transports of grief and implored her father to prevent the marriage, which Ismenor promised to do; and calling for an ugly dwarf named Rabot, he performed some spells which transported them quickly to a rocky valley through which the king and his escort were bound to pass. When the trampling of horses was heard, the magician took out an enchanted handkerchief which rendered invisible anyone who touched it. Giving one end to Rabot and holding the other himself, they walked unseen amongst the horsemen, but not a trace of Lino was to be found.

The king, tired out with exitement of the last few days, had bidden the heavy coaches, laden with presents for the princess, to go forward, while he rested under the palms with a few of his friends. Here Ismenor beheld them, all sound asleep; and casting a spell which prevented their waking till he wished them to do so, he stripped the king of all his clothes and dressed him in those of Rabot, whom he touched with his ring, saying: "Take the shape of Lino until you have wedded the daughter of the Swan fairy!"

And so great was the magicians power that Rabot believed himself to be really the king. When he had mounted Lino's horse and ridden out of sight, Ismenor aroused the king, who stared with astonishment at the dirty garments in which he was dressed. But before he had time to look about him, the magician caught him up in a cloud, and carried him off to his daughter.

In the meantime Rabot had come up with the others. "I am hungry", said he, "get me some horse's flesh, it is the best meat in the world." The steward could hardly believe his ears. King Lino was so delicate in his appetite that he lived mostly on fruit and salad.

By the time the procession reached the Swan fairy's capital there were no more horses left. The Swan fairy and her daughter awaited them on a low balcony, under which the king stopped.

"Madam", he said, "you may be surprised that I have come to ask your daughters hand in so unceremonious a fashion. But the journey is long and I was hungry and ate my horse; and I forced my courtiers to eat theirs also. Where is Hermosa?" – "Sire", answered the queen, not a little displeased as well as amazed at the kings manner, "you have my daughters portrait, and it can have made but little impression on you if you don't recognize her at once."

"I don't remember any portrait", replied Rabot. He turned to the princess, who stood there blushing and angry, and said: "If it is you, you will do very well. Let us have the wedding as soon as possible. And meantime I should like to go to sleep, after walking so far I am tired." And without waiting for a reply he bade one of the pages conduct him to his room, where he was soon snoring so loud that he could be heard at the other end of the town.

The poor princess flung herself into her mothers arms and burst into tears. The Swan fairy was so bewildered that she was almost speechless. King Lino's chamberlain begged her for a private audience, and no sooner were they alone than he told her that he feared that his master had suddenly gone mad, or had fallen under the spell of some magician. "Perhaps, madam", said he, "your fairy gifts may be able to discover the deeper meaning of this change in one whose courtesy was the talk of the kingdom." And with a low bow he took his departure.

The queen went to a secret room and going to an old chest, she drew from it a small mirror. In this mirror she could see faithfully reflected whatever she wished, and at this moment she desired above all things to behold king Lino as he really was.

Ah! the chamberlain was right! It was not Lino who was lying on his bed snoring till the palace shook beneath him. Her real son-in-law was imprisoned in one of Ismenors towers, and kissing the portrait of Hermosa. Calling her daughter, she bade her also look into the mirror, and Hermosa had the pleasure of gazing on Lino, who was behaving exactly as she could have wished. Both mother and daughter now saw the door of the prison open, and there entered the hidious Riquette, who seemed to be begging from Lino some favour, which he refused to grant. The angry woman then ordered some men to scourge the king till he fainted. Hermosa nearly dropped the mirror, but her mother caught it in time.

"Control yourself, my child", said the fairy, "we have need of all our wits if we are to rescue the king. But first it is necessary to know who the man really is that has taken his name and his face." The glass gave back the vision of a dirty, greasy little dwarf.

"So this is the trick Ismenor is hoping to play on us! We must be very careful not to let him guess that he has not deceived us, for his skill in magic is greater than mine, and I shall have to be very prudent. To begin with, I must leave you, and if the false king asks why, then answer that I had to settle some affairs on the borders of my kingdom. Meanwhile, be sure to treat him most politely and arrange fêtes to amuse him. Farewell!"

Having thus spoken the Swan fairy waved her hand, and a cloud came down and concealed her, and nobody imagined that the beautiful white cloud that was blown so rapidly across the sky was the chariot that was carrying the Swan fairy to the tower of Ismenor. Changing herself into a swallow, she began to fly round the tower till she discovered the window of Lino's prison. She flew right in, and changing shape once again, she told the king how he could free himself. Meanwhile Ismenor went into the closet where all his spells were worked, and in a short time he discovered that the Swan fairy was at that moment inside his palace. His fury was terrible. He cursed the fairy and all her subjects, turning them into stones, sparing only Hermosa. Entering the kings prison, he cried in a terrible voice: "You shall be a parrot and remain one until you can persuade Hermosa to crush you head."

He had hardly finished this sentence before a blue parrot flew out into the forest, and the magician, mounting his winged chariot, set off for the kingdom of the Swan fairy. He ordered the unhappy princess into his chariot, and in a few minutes they reached the Forest of Wonders. Here the magician got down, and dragging Hermosa out after him he said: "You are to become a tree, and a tree you will be until you have crushed the head of the person you love. But I will leave you your memory, so that your tortures may be increased."

Ismenor could not have invented a more terrible fate if he had tried for a hundred years. The hours passed wearily for the poor princess. How were they to be delivered from their doom?

The blue parrot flew about the forest, making friends, till, one day, he entered the castle of a great wizard who had just married a lovely young wife. Grenadine, for such was her name, was delighted to have a playfellow, so she took good care of the parrot. The wizard soon suspected that his wife's pet was enchanted, and he fetched his books and searched them, and found that the blue bird was really a king who had fallen under the wrath of a black magician. Eagerly he read on, looking for some means to break the enchantment, and at last, to his great joy, he discovered the remedy. Then he hurried to his wife, who was lying under a tree on which the parrot had perched, and informed her that her beloved bird was really a king and that, if she would whistle for him, they would all go to the Forest of Wonders and restore him to his own shape. Grenadine jumped up in an instant, so delighted was she, and began to whistle the song that the parrot loved. He flew down from the tree and lighted on her shoulder.

They all got into a golden boat, which carried them into the forest. The wise wizard soon found the tree he was looking for and said to his wife: "I need this tree for my magic fire. You must put he parrot on that branch and go yourself to a little distance."

The parrot remembered the prophecy of Ismenor and held himself ready, his heart beating at the thought that in this tree he beheld Hermosa. Meanwhile the wizard loosened the earth around the roots of the tree. When the parrot observed it totter and fall, he flew right under it. There was a crash; then Lino and Hermosa stood facing each other, clasped hand in hand.

The very same day Ismenor's daughter poisoned her father, and as he lay dying the Swan fairy and all her people came back to life. No magician can work spells which last beyond his own life. King Lino married

Hermosa, and Rabot got rid of his dirty clothes and bad manners and became a faithful servant to the Swan fairy.

And here we must bid them all farewell, feeling sure they will have many years of happiness after the terrible trials through which they have passed.

The massive 40-volume collection of fairytales called "Cabinet des Fées" was written over a period of 100 years in France and published by Charles-Joseph Chevalier de Mayer (1751–1825).

The Blue Parrot is a literary fairytale, but the model of a fairy-tale is in most cases a magic folktale that was once told around a fire in wintertime, its origin unknown and far back in a timeless realm. The story of king Lino is at first a pretty event of courtly love. All goes well until his neighbour Ismenor enters the scene. Then everything that was simple and straightforward becomes twisted and quite incredibly complicated. Ismenor is a magician of false power. The only good thing about him is his love for his daughter. But she is ugly like his deeds, and indeed our actions are in a way our children, we are responsible for them and they often run away from us and aquire a life of their own.

What is more mighty, good or evil? It seems in heaven the answer would be "good" and on earth "evil". Why else would Satan promise Christ the world if the latter could bring himself to kneel before him? If Satan owns the world then evil clearly rules on earth. But Satan is the father of lies. His promises are empty. Evil may be far more spectacular and impressive than good, but it has no lifeforce of its own. A black magician needs blood sacrifices because he has to steal the life of others in order to work his spells. He is not creative, so he needs to steal the fire of someone who is. There is only one almighty power in heaven and on earth and all through the known and the unknown universe: Love.

But still, most people consider an evil magician a person to be reckoned with. Maybe rightly so. Temporarily. If we have something to lose or something we want very much. Evil can destroy, mislead, kill, confuse, sabotage, delay, hurt, torture, rape, abuse, shatter, explode, irritate, rot, corrupt, reject, humiliate, discourage, steal, frighten, terrorize, agonise, control, manipulate, and as I said before: lie. All this and much more without the least bit of insight. Evil is completely ignorant, barren, empty. And yet our fairytale claims that the black magician has more power than the Swan fairy. At first, it appears to be so.

The Swan fairy of Burma, Aung San Suu Kyi, who fights for democratic freedom for her people, at first glance seems to have far less power than the corrupt military government of her country. But she is undoubtedly a highly intelligent woman, and she would not have given up her children and kept going even in prison for so many years if her goal could not be reached. On the face of it, she would have every cause to fear her opponents, but she quite obviously doesn't. Aung San Suu Kyi is a bright light for her people in a dark time.

A good example of a wizard of false power is Hitler. But for a long time it did look VERY bleak when he had taken over most of Europe. The chances of defeating the Germans seemed to many almost nil. So soon after the first world war, no country exept Germany was ready for another. And yet England was willing to fight Hitler, even after the occupation of France and before the US army joined them.

One of the dangers of black magic is its seductiveness. Sarah Mearns, principal dancer of the New York City Ballet, says about Odile, the evil witch in "Swan Lake": "She is completely selfish and does not care about the prince's feelings. You don't want to be this person. But it is fun! It feels powerful! She does not only fool the prince, she fools the entire audience!" But such trickery has nothing to do with power. It says in our fairytale: "So great was the magician Ismenor's power that the dwarf Rabot believed himself to really be the king." To drive the poor dwarf insane is hardly a great feat. The Swan fairy is in a predicament only because she has made a commitment to act in accordance with cosmic laws.

She cannot lie or cheat and much less kill and remain her true self at the same time. She cannot and will not do any harm to anyone.

The Christian hymn "Amazing grace, how sweet the sound, that saved a wretch like me!" was written by the slavetrader John Newton after he and his ship had survived a violent storm. His poetic outburst did not, however, prevent him from still being heavily involved with the Atlantic slave trade for six more years. Maybe, coming out of that terrible storm, it should have dawned on him that he no longer had the excuse of being a wretch and that the black people of Africa were no wretches either! It feels so safe and it is so cheap to simply hide behind a confession of being bad, unworthy, and generally inadequate. It's certainly the easy way out. It was the burden of being a supreme Being of Light that made Christ one of the greatest healers on earth. It is high time for us to be willing to share this burden! Not to be crowned with thorns and nailed to a cross, but to be crowned with stars like his mother Maria and to initiate the All Healing and Ascension process of our planet together with her. One day even the last of the dark spirits that haunt us will return to the source of love and light eternal, and since in actual fact there is no linear time, this day is NOW, and we might as well act on it!

The false king Lino is eating his horse. In Arabia horses are known to come from the stars and often have names of stars. Like the ancient celts, the Arabs used to sleep beside their horses. You can do this only if a horse trusts you completely. Otherwise the horse will not lie down to sleep and remain standing all night. It is therefore impossible for a king of Arabia to slaughter his precious horses. In any case, to kill a horse (or any other animal) and to eat it, is a crime, whether we like it or not.

As the real Lino flies around as a blue parrot and the Swan fairy is turned into a statue and her daughter into a tree in the forest of wonders, we encounter a true magician. He is eager to help and is naturally baffled by the prophecy that the princess Hermosa must crush the head of her beloved in order to transform him into his human form. Practitioners of black magic all over the world gain control by killing what is most precious to them. So the curse that fell on the princess Hermosa is an open invitation for her to become an evil witch. The only way out of this dilemma is to create a situation in which the tree is made to fall and the blue parrot can sacrifice himself without coercion, through his free will. That the spells of a sorcerer do not last longer than his life is not always true. I have asked my guides and angels to unravel curses that went back hundreds and sometimes thousands of years. They have to take the life-force out of the spells or curses, clear it and restore it to the universe. After that we attend to the healing that is needed. It is a lengthy process.

The women are rather passive in the French fairytale of the Blue Parrot. The Swan fairy makes an attempt to set the king free and is promptly made immobile. The action is left to the two magicians. "I wish a woman could have action in her life like a man!" says Charlotte Brontë's heroine Jane Eyre. In our present fairytale this sentence must remain wishful thinking.

A nice contrast to the "Blue Parrot" is the famous German fairytale of "Dornröschen" ("Sleeping Beauty"). Here the princess Rose or Aurora appears as a very precious, long awaited heir to the throne, her birth heralded and prophecized to the queen by the nature kingdom. A magic christening follows, with blessings from the wise women of the realm. In the ballet version the young princess is wooed by four princes, but she does not choose a consort. Her celebrated balancing act, standing on one leg on point and giving her hand to each of her suitors in turn, but remaining beautifully poised and seemingly weightless all by herself in between, is a confirmation of her great inner strength. She belongs to herself. She is the shining star of the kingdom, and when she falls asleep for a hundred years, her godmother, the lilac fairy, whose power transformed death into a lovely dream, protects her and leads her bridegroom to her.

The empire of king Lino seems strangely unreal. His story unfolds almost like a puppet show. Even the magic, plentiful as it is, lacks conviction. Poetry is not something decorative. It is the white flame of divine truth, awesome and inspiring. Ancient stories stay alive for a reason. Myths and fairytales can uncover dangerous lies, and they can also show us the way home to the stars where we came from.

The Death of Koshchei the Deathless

From Russia

In a certain kingdom there lived a prince Ivan. He had three sisters. The first was the princess Marya, the second the princess Olga, the third the princess Anna. When their father and mother lay at the point of death, they had thus enjoined their son: "Give your sisters in marriage to the first suitors who come to woo them. Don't go keeping them by you."

They died, and the prince buried them, and then to solace his grief, he went with his sisters into the garden. Suddenly the sky was covered by a black cloud; a terrible storm arose. "Let us go home, sisters!" he cried. Hardly had they got into the palace, when the thunder pealed, the ceiling split open, and into the room came flying a Falcon bright. The Falcon smote upon the ground, became a brave youth, and said: "Hail, prince Ivan! Before I came as a guest, but now I have come as a wooer! I wish to propose for your sister, the princess Marya."

"If you find favour in the eyes of my sister, I will not interfere with her wishes." The princess Marya gave her consent; the Falcon married her and bore her away into his own realm.

A year later prince Ivan and his two sisters went out to stroll in the garden. Again there arose a storm-cloud with whirlwind and lightning. "Let us go home, sisters!" cried the prince. Scarcely had they entered the palace, when the thunder crashed, the roof burst into a blaze, the ceiling split in twain, and in flew an Eagle. He smote upon the ground and became a brave youth. "Hail, prince Ivan! Before I came as a guest, but now I come as a wooer!" He asked for the hand of the princess Olga.

"If you find favour with my sister, then let her marry you." The princess Olga married the Eagle, and he carried her off into his kingdom.

Another year went by. Prince Ivan was in the garden with his youngest sister. Again a storm arose and they went into the palace just when the thunder crashed; the ceiling burst open and in flew a Raven, smote upon the floor and became a brave youth.

"Well, prince Ivan, before I came as a guest, and now I have come as a wooer. Give me the princess Anna to wife!" – "I won't interfere with my sisters freedom. If you gain her affections, let her marry you."

So the princess Anna married the Raven and went with him into his own realm. Prince Ivan lived alone for a while; then he grew weary and said: "I will go out in search of my sisters."

He got ready for the journey, he rode and rode, and one day he saw a whole army lying dead on the plain. He cried aloud: "If there be a living man there, let him make answer. Who has slain this mighty host?" There replied unto him a living man: "All this mighty host has been slain by the princess Morevna."

Prince Ivan rode further on and came to a white tent, and forth came to meet him the fair princess Morevna.

"Hail prince", said she, "If your business be not pressing, tarry a while in my tent." Prince Ivan was glad to spend the night in the tent, and he found favour in the eyes of the princess, and she married him and carried him off into her own realm.

They spent some time together, and then the princess took it into her head to go to war. So she handed over all the house-keeping affairs to prince Ivan and gave him those instructions: "Go about everywhere, keep watch over everything; only do not venture to look into that closet there."

He couldn't help doing so. The moment princess Morevna had gone, he rushed to the closet, pulled open the door and looked in – there hung Koshchei the Deathless, fettered by twelve chains. Then Koshchei entreated prince Ivan: "Have pity upon me and give me to drink! Ten long years I have been here in torment, neither eating nor drinking; my throat is utterly dried up."

The prince gave him a bucketful of water, he drank it up and asked for more. The prince gave him a second bucketful. Koshchei drank it up and asked for a third, and when he had swallowed it, he regained his former strenth, gave his chains a shake, and broke all twelve at once.

"Thanks, prince Ivan!" cried Koshchei the Deathless, "now you will sooner see your own ears than princess Morevna!" and out of the window he flew in the shape of a terrible whirlwind. And he came up with the princess Morevna, laid hold of her and carried her off to his home. Prince Ivan wept full sore, and then he set out, saying to himself: "Whatever happens I will go and look for Morevna!"

After some days on the road he saw a wonderous palace, and by the side of the palace stood an oak tree, and on the oak tree sat a Falcon bright. Down flew the Falcon from the oak, smote upon the ground, turned into a brave youth and cried aloud: "Ha, dear brother in law! How is it with you?" Out came running the princess Marya and joyfully greeted her brother. Prince Ivan spent three days with them; then he said: "I cannot abide with you; I must go and search for my wife." The Falcon told him to leave his silver spoon with them. They would look at it and remember him.

On went prince Ivan, and by dawn of the third day he saw a palace still grander then the former one and by its side an oak tree, and on it sat an Eagle. Down flew the Eagle, smote upon the ground, turned into a brave youth, and cried aloud: "Rise up, princess Olga! Hither comes our brother dear!" The princess Olga immediatly ran to meet him and kiss him. Again, prince Ivan stopped with them for three days, then he said: "I cannot stay here any longer. I am going to look for my wife." The Eagle entreated him to leave his silver fork with them. He did it and went his way until he saw a palace grander than the first two, and near the palace an oak tree and on it a Raven. Down flew the Raven from the oak, smote upon the ground, turned into a brave youth and cried aloud: "Princess Anna, come forth quickly! Our brother is here!" Out ran the princess Anna, embracing him and asking after his health. Prince Ivan stayed for three days with them, then he went to look for his wife, leaving his silver snuff-box behind.

After a long time he found Morevna. She flung her arms around his neck, burst into tears, and exclaimed: "Oh, prince Ivan! Why did you disobey me, looking into the closet and letting out Koshchei the Deathless?" – "Forgive me, Morevna. Fly with me while Koshchei the Deathless is out of sight!"

So they got ready and fled. Now Koshchei was out hunting. Towards evening he was returning home, when his good steed stumbled beneath him. "Why stumblest thou? Scentest thou some ill?" The steed replied: "Prince Ivan has come and carried off Morevna." – "Is it possible to catch them?" – "It is possible to sow wheat, to wait till it grows up, to reap it and thresh it, to ground it to flour, to make a pie and eat it, and then to start in persuit – and even then to be in time."

Koshchei galloped off and caught up with prince Ivan. "Now"", says he, "this time I will forgive you, in return for your kindness in giving me water to drink. And a second time I will forgive you; but the third time beware! I will cut you to bits."

Then he took Morevna and carried her off. But prince Ivan sat down on a stone and burst into tears. He wept and wept – and then returned back to Morevna. They got ready and fled, and Koshchei the Deathless caught up with them again. He forgave prince Ivan, but when he came after him and Morevna for the third time, he chopped him into little pieces, put them into a barrel, and flung it into the blue sea.

At that very time the silver articles which Prince Ivan had left behind with his brothers-in-laws turned black.

"Ah!" they said, "the evil is accomplished sure enough!" Then the Eagle hurried to the blue sea, caught hold of the barrel, and dragged it ashore; the Falcon flew away for the Water of Life, and the Raven for the Water of Death. Afterwards they all three met, broke open the barrel, took out the remains of prince Ivan, washed them and put them together in fitting order. The Raven sprinkled them with the Water of Death – the pieces joined together and the body became whole. The Falcon sprinkled it with the Water of Life – prince Ivan shuddered, stood up and said: "Ah! What a time I have been sleeping!"

"You would have gone on sleeping a good deal longer if it had not been for us", replied his brothers-in-law, and they gave him this advice: "Find out where Koshchei the Deathless got so good a steed!"

When prince Ivan met his wife again, he asked her to approach Koshchei the Deathless in a favourable moment with this question. This she did, and Koshchei said: "Beyond thrice nine lands, on the other side of the fiery river, there lives Baba Yaga. She has so good a mare that she flies right round the world with it every day. And she has many other splendid mares."

"But how did you get across the fiery river?"

"Why, I have a handkerchief of this kind – when I wave it thrice, there springs up a very lofty bridge, and the fire cannot reach it."

Morevna did listen to all this, and repeated it to prince Ivan, and she took the handkerchief and gave it to him. So he went on his way through thrice nine lands and managed to get across the fiery river and tried to find Baba Yaga. Long went he on without getting anything either to eat or to drink. At last he saw an outlandish bird and its young ones. He said: "I will eat one of these chickens."

"Don't eat my young ones, prince Ivan!" begged the outlandish bird, "some time or other I will do you a good turn."

The prince went on farther and saw a hive of bees in the forest. "I will get a bit of honeycomb", said he.

"Don't disturb my honey, prince Ivan!" exclaimed the queen bee, "some time or other I'll do you a good turn."

So he did not disturb it and went on. Presently there met him a lioness with her cub.

"I am so hungry, I will eat this lion cub!" said he. "Please leave us alone, prince Ivan!" begged the lioness, "some time or other I'll do you a good turn."

Hungry and faint he wandered on, walked father and farther, and at last found the house of Baba Yaga. Round the house were set twelve poles in a circle, and on each of eleven of these was stuck a human head. The twelfth alone remained unoccupied.

"Hail, grandmother!"
"Hail, prince Ivan! Wherefore have you come?"

"I have come to earn from you a heroic steed." – "So be it, prince! If you take good care of my mares for three days, I will give you what you are asking for. But if you don't, you will find your head stuck on top of the last pole up there."

Prince Ivan agreed to these terms. Baba Yaga gave him food and drink and bade him set about his business. But the moment he had driven the mares afield, they cocked up their tails, and away they tore across the meadows in all directions. Before the prince had time to look around they were all out of sight. Thereupon he began to weep, and then he sat down and went to sleep. But when the sun was near its setting the outlandish bird came flying up to him, and awakened him, saying: "Arise, prince Ivan, the mares are at home now."

The Prince returned to Baba Yaga who was storming and raging at her mares, and shrieking: "Whatever did you come home for?"

"How could we help coming home? There came flying birds from every part of the world, and all but pecked our eyes out!"

"Well, well. Tomorrow don't go galloping over the meadows, but disperse amid the thick forests."

The next day the prince drove the mares afield once more. Immediately they cocked up their tails and dispersed among the thick forests. Again did the prince sit down and weep and weep, and then go to sleep. The sun set down behind the forest. Up came running the lioness.
"Arise, prince Ivan! The mares are all collected."

Prince Ivan went back to Baba Yaga, who more than ever stormed at her mares, and shrieked: "Whatever did you come home for?"

"How could we help coming home? Beasts of prey came running at us from all parts of the world, and all but tore us to pieces!"
"Well, tomorrow run off into the blue sea!"

Next morning for the last time did prince Ivan drive the mares afield, who cocked up their tails and fled into the blue sea. There they stood up to their necks in water. Prince Ivan wept and fell asleep. But just before sunset, up came flying a bee and said: "Arise, Prince! The mares are all collected. But when you go back, don't let Baba Yaga set eyes on you! Go into the stable and hide behind the mangers. There you will find a sorry colt rolling in the muck. Take it, and at the dead of night ride away from the house."

Prince Ivan slipped into the stable and lay down behind the mangers, while Baba Yaga was shrieking at her mares: "Why did you come back?"

"There came flying bees in countless numbers from all parts of the world and began stinging till the blood came." Baba Yaga went to sleep. In the dead of the night prince Ivan took the sorry colt, jumped on its back and galloped away to the fiery river. There he waved the handkerchief three times and rode across the bridge. He waved the hand-kerchief twice only on the other side; there remained a thin, ever so thin bridge.

When Baba Yaga got up in the morning the sorry colt was not to be seen. Off she went in pursuit. Halfway across the fiery river, the bridge broke and Baba Yaga met with a cruel death.

Prince Ivan fattened the colt in the green meadows and it turned into a wondrous steed. Then he rode to where Morevna was. She cried: "By what means did you come back to life?" He told her everything and they rode away together. Koshchei the Deathless found out what had happened, went after the fugitives and after a long while came up with them. He wanted to kill them, but prince Ivans horse smote Koshchei full swing with its hoof and cracked his skull. Afterwards the prince heaped up a pile of wood, burned Koshcheis dead body and scattered his ashes to the wind. Morevna mounted Koshchei's horse, prince Ivan got on his own, and they rode away to visit the Raven, the Eagle and the Falcon.

In this fairytale the Dragons Mother (see "The Flower Queen's Daughter", p. 15) becomes Baba Yaga. In both cases the hero must look after the magic horses for three days. Both the Dragon Mother and Baba Yaga are meant to be symbols of evil. Another word for dragon is Satan. As I wrote before, a real dragon is a wonderful being of light and a guardian of cosmic power. Baba Yaga is, like Kali in India, an earth goddess. Kali has a necklace of skulls around her neck, Baba Yaga has a circle of human heads around her house, tokens of death. Kali is the fierce aspect of the compassionate goddess Durga, who represents the ultimate salvation of Earth. In spite of her ferocious appearance, Kali's devotees have a very loving and intimate relationship with her. They become her children and she is the ever-caring great mother. The god Shiva, her consort, is also called Kala, the eternal time. In Slavic folklore Baba Yaga is a distinctive and many-faceted figure. She can be very helpful and also very destructive. Baba means woman, or specifically, old woman. Babushka is a grandmother in Russia. The meaning of the word "Yaga" is unclear. It could be related to the sanskrit word for serpent. Hence her transformation into the Dragons Mother or vice versa. A dragon is often seen as a flying or feathered serpent like Quetzalcoatl or Kukulcan, the god of the morning and evening star (Venus), a major deity of the ancient Mexican pantheon, the patron of priests and the inventor of books and of the famous Mayan calendar.

Russia was christianized from Greece. Some of the grand princes and Tsars married princesses from Byzantium, who brought their religion and their icons along with them. Now both Russia and Greece abound with icons, many of whom are working miracles, since every icon is a living saint. The heart prayer of the monks on mount Athos: "Kyrios, Jesu Christe, eleison!" was meditated by pilgrims on all the streets in Russia until the revolution made an end of it. Of course the patriarchs of Moscow, who were the head of the Greek Orthodox church in Russia, did not take kindly to Baba Yaga, so she got a bad press and was labelled as evil. But Baba Yaga is really associated with empowerment. Her horses are all-knowing and their energy is boundless. The mare that flies round the world with her every day is the sun, so Baba Yaga is also an ancient sun-goddess.

Prince Ivan is a very emotional man. In Switzerland we would say: "He has built his house close to the water". Otherwise this fairytale is heavily imprinted with the element air. In another slavic fairytale three sisters marry the three winds, and here they are wedded to the king and the masters of air and wind, the eagle, the falcon and the raven. They all appear with a thunderstorm and damage the roof of the palace, proof of enomous strength.

Prince Ivan's sisters marry into the bird klan. If we connect deeply with nature, we can escape the prison of conceptual thinking and reach a wisdom that is limitless. We can spread our wings and fly. No nature being that is left alone by humans understands our language because it really is a language of war. Words like "surrender", "win", "dominance", "separation", "competition", "resistance" are meaningless in nature. All our sentences are at least tinged with the ghost of armed altercation. Peace means only a temporary suspension of hostilities.

A gross and silly proverb like "all is fair in love and war" is simply a license to behave like a cad, apart from the fact that to mix up love with war like that most truly gives the show away. A tree or a stone or a bird speaks directly from the heart like the stars in the sky. It speaks in silence, and this silence is a sweet, serene stillness that is beyond words. Music and poetry can come close to this speaking stillness, which is why bards long ago had magic powers and could influence the elements. The princess Morevna defeats an entire army on her own and then carries off her bridgroom like an amazon queen. She belongs to the last phase of the matriarchy, when women had to fight men to defend their authority. She speaks the language of war with distinction, which explains why Koshchei the Deathless is bound up with twelve chains in her closet. She has resemblance to Bluebeard, and naturally the poor Prince MUST open the forbidden closet just like the victims of the bluebearded serial killer HAVE TO open the door to their doom. To go to war without very serious threats to freedom and safety and to all that is good and true is a crime. And just like a serial killer becomes addicted to his bloody business, so has the Princess Morevna become addicted to war. War overcame our planet like a terrible virus, and this vicious and merciless illness spread like wildfire all around the globe.

But who IS Koshchei the Deathless? Is he this virus of war I have been talking of? Is this why he has power over princess Morevna? You can starve a virus, but it is not easy to kill it, and the moment it is fed, it will indeed break all chains, as we could see when the Spanish flu broke out at the end of World War One, killing millions of people, or the corona 19 virus in our present time. What is Koshcheis' connection to Baba Yaga, since he is riding one of her horses? Wait and see.

The three birds that married the three sisters of Prince Ivan have power over life and death. The Falcon bright, who has the Water of Life, reminds us of Horus, the beautiful Egyptian god of the sun and the sky, the son or in other traditions the brother of Isis. The Raven, who has the Water of Death, is clearly linked with the celtic raven goddess of death, Morrigu, the phantom queen. The Eagle sits in the East of the medicine wheel and represents the pneuma, the holy breath or creator spirit and the fire from heaven, enlightenment. Why is the dead body of prince Ivan first sprinkled with the Water of Death? A shaman can get his initiation through death and transformation. His body can lie under water for many days and still come back to life. I too was cut into little pieces like prince Ivan in a shamanistic journey, and it was most helpful to me to become pure bones and later to be given a new body and begin anew. Even in a convent a nun is asked to let her old existence pass away completely. She is given a new name and a new family in Christ. Prince Ivan needs this initiation through death in order to cross the fiery river, to endure hunger and thirst and learn compassion with his animal brothers and sisters, to learn their language, to find Baba Yaga and finally get one of her magic horses.

Baba Yaga belongs to a time long before Buddha, Quan Yin and Christ declared a faith that embodied compassion and love. Her creed is based on survival. As long as we fight to survive we cannot hear or understand the glad tidings of good things that the angels of peace bring to us. The very word survival makes it impossible to embrace life fully. It carries the seed of death, and what is worse, the fear of death. And yet it is so much better to die at once than to live in fear. What I mean is: if we did not fear death or if we understood clearly that our physical bodies can either decay or ascend, but that life is always and everywhere eternal, we would be better off. We would actually HAVE a life and not just sit out a period of very limited time until the grim reaper walks in on us. My admiration for the French writer Colette is very sincere. Her mastery of language often takes my breath away. But she is obsessed with youth and a dread of old age. In her eyes, only the young are beautiful. An old person is quite literally a monster for Colette.

There are quite a few persons who I consider to have become far more beautiful as they grew older and even very old. The wonderful actor Burt Lancaster in the movies "Il Gattopardo" or "Conversation Piece" is ten times more handsome and attractive than he was thirty or forty years earlier in his career. I had master classes with Nadja Boulanger when she was in her eighties. I never met a more graceful, wise or beautiful woman than her. She is one of two leading lights among humans in my spiritual life. The other is my neighbour here in Ireland, Sonny. Both were basically very simple and had no respect whatsoever for hierarchies. Sonny was around seventy when I first met him and the most contented man you could imagine. When I visited him on Christmas-Eve he sat beside the fire with his tea. He had one candle in the window to welcome the holy family. Nothing else. No special food, no presents, no decoration and no greenery of any kind. But he was perfectly happy.

Once I met him on the mountain in fierce and foul weather. The rain came down in buckets into our faces. Sonny wore only a thin coat that was certainly not weatherproof. He smiled at me and said: "It is very rough. But no matter. No matter." Whenever I met a really conceited would-be guru and temporarily lost faith in the esoteric society, I had only to think of Sonny to be instantly comforted and secure in myself. Sonny was more than ninety years of age when he left his physical body behind. About a month before he passed over he told me that, as a lad, he had been sent to look after the horses and see to it they would not get into the bog. As he got near the swamp, he noticed another farmer who had already driven the horses out of danger. It was his neighbour in his Sunday best who had died a week earlier. When Sony told me this, I knew I could count on him to be still around after his death, if we needed him, in his Sunday best, looking after us, humans and beasts and plants.

Baba Yaga and Koshchei are in a way related. They can both be perfectly loathsome. Baba Yaga makes a promise to prince Ivan, but she does not honour it. She does not give him one of her horses, he has to steal it in the dead of the night, and it is a sorry colt rolling in the muck. However, in the world of magic muck is often pure gold, and the sorry colt has the amazing power to kill the deathless.

Prince Ivan married an addict. Trying to rescue an addict is often like pouring water into a leaky vessel. To keep an addiction in a closet is a good metapher for the fact that almost all addicts will deny their addiction or even be oblivious of it. But the addiction can run faster than lightning to catch a poor devil who tries to get away from it. Koshchei the Deathless embodies both the virus to cause the fatal illness and the illness itself. But prince Ivan is detemined to help and to free his wife. His path is a dangerous one. The twelfth pole in the circle round Baba Yaga's house has an ominous signifcance. It is clearly waiting for the head of prince Ivan. Without the help of the animals the prince would be done for. They do all the work for him. All he does is weep and sleep. As a powerful healer once said, life can be ninety percent miraculous, nine percent magic and only one percent work.

As soon as we become fully aware of all the great and the small miracles that occur every day, we are on our way. We don't even have to weep. But sleeping and above all lucid dreaming can be most helpful and effective. It can encourage the Wu Wei, the doing without doing, the action of non-action, one of Taoism's most important concepts. Being one with the flow of life. Victor Marie Hugo, the great French poet of the Romantic movement, said: "There is nothing like a dream to create the future."

That Baba Yaga and Koshchei the Deathless are both burned to cinders is a nice touch by the Russian patriarchs. But of course the old witch is still alive and kicking, and her magic horses cock up their tails and run free on the green meadows, in the thick forests, the blue sea and among the clouds of heaven.

Kupti and Imani

A Punjabi story

Once there was a king who had two daughters; and their names were Kupti and Imani. He loved them both very much, and spent hours talking to them, and one day he said to Kupti, the elder: "Are you satisfied to leave your life and your fortunes in my hands?"

"Verily, yes", answered the princess, surprised at the question. "In whose hands should I leave them, if not yours?"

But when he asked his younger daughter Imani the same question, she replied: "No indeed! If I had a chance I would make my own fortune!"

At this answer the king was very displeased and said: "You are too young to know the meaning of your words. But, be it so; I will give you the chance of gratifying your wish."

Then he sent for an old lame fakir who lived in a tumbledown hut on the outskirts of the city, and when he had presented himself, the king said: "You are very old and nearly crippled, you would be glad for some young person to live with you and serve you; so I will send you my young daughter. She wants to earn her living, and she can do so with you."

Of course the old fakir had not a word to say, or, if he had, he was really too astonished and troubled to say it. But the young princess went off with him smiling and tripped along quite gaily, whilst he hobbled home with her in perplexed silence.

When they got to the hut the fakir began to think what he could arrange for the princess's comfort. But after all he was a fakir, and his house was bare except for one bedstead, an old cooking pot and an earthen jar for water. However, the princess soon ended his perplexity by asking: "Have you any money?"

"I have a penny somewhere", replied the fakir. "Very well", rejoined the princess, "take the penny and go out and borrow me a spinning-wheel and a loom."

After much seeking, the fakir found the penny and started on his errand, whilst the princess went off shopping. First she bought a farthing's worth of oil, and then she bought three farthing's worth of flax. When she got back with her purchases, she set the old man on the bedstead and rubbed his crippled leg with the oil for an hour. Then she sat down to the spinning-wheel and spun and spun all night long, whilst the old man slept, until, in the morning, she had spun the finest thread that ever was seen. Next she went to the loom and wove and wove until, by the evening, she had woven a beautiful silver cloth.

"Now", said she to the fakir, when she had finished, "go to the marketplace and sell my cloth while I rest."

"And what am I to ask for it?" said the old man. "Two gold pieces", replied the princess.

So the fakir hobbled away and stood in the marketplace to sell the cloth. At just that time the elder princess drove by, and when she saw the cloth she stopped and asked the price.

"Two gold pieces", said the fakir, and the princess gladly paid them, after which the fakir went home with the money.

Imani continued as she had done before, day after day. Always she spent a penny upon oil and tended the old man's lame leg. Gradually the city became famous for her beautiful cloth, the old fakir's lame leg became straighter and stronger, and the hole under the floor of the hut where they kept their money became fuller and fuller of gold pieces. At last the princess said: "I really think we have got enough to live in greater comfort." And she sent for builders who built a beautiful house for her and the old fakir, and in all the city there was none finer except the kings palace. Presently, this reached the ears of the king, and when he inquired whose it was, he was told it belonged to his daughter.

„Well", exclaimed the king, "she said she would make her own fortune, and somehow or other she seems to have done it."

A little while after this, business took the king to another country, and before he went, he asked his elder daughter what she would like him to bring her back as a gift.

"A necklace of rubies", she answered. And then the king thought he would like to ask Imani, too. So he sent a messenger to find out what sort of present she wanted. The man happened to arrive just as she was trying to disentangle a knot in her loom, and bowing low before her, he said: "The king sends me to inquire what you wish him to bring you as a present from the country of Dur?" But Imani, who was only considering how she could best untie the knot without breaking the thread, replied: "Patience!" meaning that the messenger should wait till she was able to attend to him. But the messenger went off with this as an answer, and told the king that the only thing the princess Imani wanted was "patience."

"Oh!" said the king, "I don't know whether this is a thing to be bought in Dur; I never had it myself, but if it is to be got, I will buy it for her."

Next day the king departed on his journey, and when his business in Dur was completed, he bought for Kupti a beautiful ruby necklace. Then he said to the servant: "The princess Imani wants some patience. You must go to the market and inquire, and if any is to be sold, get it and bring it to me."

The servant saluted and left the king's presence. He walked about the market for some time, crying: "Has anyone patience to sell? Patience to sell?" Some of the people mocked, some told him to go away, and some said: "The fellow is mad!" At length it came to the ears of the king of Dur that there was a madman in the market trying to buy patience. The king laughed and said: "I should like to see the fellow! Bring him here!"

Immediately his attendants went to seek the man and brought him to the king, who asked: "What is this you want?" – "Sire, I am bidden to ask for patience." – "Oh", said the king, "you must have a strange master! What does he want with it?" – "My master wants it for his daughter Imani." – "I know of some patience which the young lady might have if she cares for it. But it is not to be bought."

Now the name of the king was Subbar Khan, and Subbar means "patience"; but the messenger did not know that, or understand that the king was making a joke. However, he declared that the princess Imani was not only young and beautiful, but also the most clever, industrious and kind-hearted of princesses; and he would have gone on extolling her virtues had not the king laughingly put up his hand and stopped him, saying: "Well, well, wait a minute and I will see what can be done."

With that he got up and went to his own apartments and took out a little casket. Into this he put a fan, and, shutting it carefully, he brought it to the messenger and said: "Here is a casket. It has no lock or key and will open only to the touch of the person who needs its contents – and whoever opens it will obtain patience. But I can't tell you whether it will be quite the kind of patience that is wanted."

The servant bowed low and took the casket. He gave thanks, went away and gave the casket and an account of his adventure to his master.

As soon as their father got back to his country, Kupti and Imani each got the presents he had brought for them. Imani was very surprised when the casket was given to her by the hand of the messenger.

"But", she said, "what is this? I never asked for anything! Indeed I had no time, for the messenger ran away before I had unravelled my tangle." But the servant declared that the casket was for her, so she took it with some curiosity, and brought it to the old fakir. The old man tried to open it, but in vain. He gave it to Imani, who hardly touched it before it opened quite easily, and there lay within a beautiful fan. With a cry of surprise and pleasure the princess took out the fan and began to fan herself.

Hardly had she finished three strokes of the fan before there suddenly appeared from nowhere in particular – king Subbar Khan of Dur. Imani gasped and rubbed her eyes, and the old fakir sat and gazed in such astonishment that for some time he could not speak. At length he said: "Who may you be, fair sir, if you please?"

"My name", said the king, "is Subbar Khan of Dur. This lady", bowing to the princess, "has summoned me, and here I am."

"I?" stammered the princess, "I have summoned you? I never saw you before now, so how could that be?"

Then the king told them everything that had happened. "The fan is magical", he added, "when anyone uses the fan, in three strokes of it I am with them; if they fold it and tap it on the table, in three taps I am home again. This fair lady asked for patience, and as that is my name, here I am, very much at her service."

Now the princess Imani, being highminded, was anxious to fold up the fan, and give the three taps which would send the king home again. But the old fakir was so very pleased with his guest that he bade her tarry, and they spent a pleasant evening together.

After that he was often summoned; and as both the fakir and he were fond of chess and were good players, they used to sit up half the night playing. At last one room in the house began to be called the king's room, and whenever he stayed late, he used to sleep there and go home again in the morning.

By-and-by it came to the ears of princess Kupti that there was a rich and handsome young man visiting at her sister's house, and she was very jealous. So she went one day to pay Imani a visit, and pretended to be very affectionate and interested in the house. As the sisters went from place to place, Kupti was shown Subbar Khan's room, and presently, making some excuse, she slipped in there by herself and swiftly spread over the bed a quantity of very finely powdered glass which was poisoned.

That very evening Subbar Khan came and played chess with the fakir as usual. As he lay down on the bed, the tiny splinters of poisoned glass ran into him. He soon felt as though he were burning from head to foot. He never said a word, but sat in agony all night thinking he was poisoned by Imani. When he was transported home in the morning, he sent for all the doctors in his kingdom, but none could make out what his illness was. So he lingered for weeks and weeks in pain and fever, until he was at the point of death.

Meanwhile, the princess Imani and the old fakir were much troubled because, although they waved the magic fan, no Subbar Khan appeared, and they feared that some evil fate had overtaken him. At last the princess was so anxious that she was determined to go herself to the kingdom of Dur. Disguising herself as a young fakir, she set out upon her journey alone and on foot. One evening she found herself in a forest and lay down under a tree to pass the night. Presently she heard two monkeys talking to one another in the tree above her head.

"Good evening, brother", said one, "whence come you – and what is the news?"

"I come from Dur", said the other, "and the news is, the king is dying."

"I am sorry to hear that. What is the matter with him?"

"No man knows. But the birds, who see all and carry all messages, say that he is dying of poisoned glass that princess Kupti spread upon his bed.

"That is terrible. But if they only knew it, the berries of the very tree we sit in, steeped in hot water, will cure such a disease in three days at most."

"Men are so silly. They shut themselves up in stuffy houses in stuffy cities instead of living in nice airy trees, and so they miss knowing all the best things!"

As soon as daylight dawned over the forest, Imani began to gather berries from the tree. Then she walked on as fast as she could, and in two days reached the city of Dur.

After some delay she was admitted to the palace, and, whilst she was so well disguised that the king did not recognise her, he was so wasted by illness that she hardly knew him. She asked for a pot of boiling water and steeped some of the berries in it and told the king's attendants to wash his body with it. This did so much good that the king slept quietly all night. The second day she did the same, and this time the king declared he was hungry and called for food. After the third day he was quite well, only very weak from his long illness. He sent his servants to fetch the physician who had cured him. When Imani appeared, everyone marvelled that so young a man should be so clever a doctor. The king wanted to give him all kinds of precious things. At first Imani would take nothing, but at last she said, if she must be rewarded, she would ask for the king's signet ring and his handkerchief. Then she departed and went back to her own country.

There she related all her adventures to the fakir, and a little while after they sent for Subbar Khan by means of the magic fan. They asked him why he had stayed away for so long, and he told them all about his illness and how he had been cured. When he had finished his story, the princess rose up and opening a cabinet, brought out the ring and the handkerchief and said, laughing: "Are these the rewards you gave to the doctor?"

At that the king looked, and he recognised her, and understood in a moment all that had happened. Imani told him about her sister's jealousy; and the king jumped up and put the magic fan in his pocket and asked Imani to come with him and be his wife. And so it was settled, and the old fakir and Imani went to the city of Dur, where Imani was married to the king and lived happily ever after.

The Punjabi are a clan of the Indo-Aryab people (a branch of the Indo-Iranian language), originating from Punjab (land of five waters), found between eastern Pakistan and northern India. Both Pakistan and India do not grant a lot of independence to their women. In India widows are still sometimes burned or starved or poisoned to death. And indeed the older of the two daughters of the king, Kupti, cannot imagine her life being her own. For her, her fate and her existence must be in someone else's hands.

Many of our religions mirror this view. We are at the mercy of a god, who wants to be feared and praised day and night. But, if we are truly one with our own divine self, we don't need gods or goddesses, priests and priestesses, prophets or gurus or lamas, we don't need religion. Everything we wish is within ourselves in abundance, and if there are any questions or problems that plague us, we can always find an answer or a solution by ourselves – if we own our power instead of giving it into other hands. It is interesting that the name of Imani, the younger princess who wishes to be responsible for herself, means the same as Immanuel: "the divine within."

The Punjabi king reminds us of William Shakespeare's "King Lear". He, like Lear, sends his younger daughter off without a penny because he is displeased with her. Like Lear he is used to play god almighty in his daughters' and his subjects' life. But unlike Cordelia, king Lear's youngest daughter, the princess Imani goes smiling into the exile. Whatever happens to us, it is up to us what we make of it and how we wish to react.

A fakir is a Hindu, Buddhist or Muslim Sufi ascetic, a wandering Dervish and a beggar living on alms. He has renounced all relations and possessions. The fakir in our story is too old and too lame to be wandering. He is however a good and honest man and to be trusted, and that is more than can be said of many a young and handsome husband. Princess Imani is neither his wife nor his servant, she does exactly as she pleases and answers to no-one. But like the fakir, she has a gentle disposition, and the first thing she buys is oil to tend the fakir's crippled leg. She makes good use of her gifts and soon her house is almost as fine as the king's palace, and what is best: it belongs to herself, not to her father, and it is exactly the way she likes it to be.

It is a fine example of synchronicity that Imani is asking the messenger for patience while trying to untangle a knot at the very moment her father leaves for the kingdom of a ruler whose name is Patience. It is also significant that the messenger of Imani's father who is brought before king Subbar Khan is praising her virtues. Obviously he does so because he sincerely loves and admires the princess. She has become a way-shower to her people, to the men as well as to the women.

Synchronicity is a causal connection of two or more psycho-physic phenomena. In simpler terms, it is a miracle, or a case of inner guidance for which we have no rational explanation. It happens when our angels and spiritual guides give us a nudge or a hint. King Subbar Khan is well aware of this and acts accordingly. He has acquired some advanced training in white magic and can close a casket without lock or key so that it will open only at the right moment and for the right person. He can also charm a fan so that it will summon him. It is almost like our way of using computers as telephones, only much superior to this rather complicated modern method.

Even the fakir has no power over the casket. But he is such a sweet and gentle soul that not only does he welcome Imani's mysterious suitor, he is so very pleased with him, he makes him stay all evening. He knows no jealousy. But Kupti does. The life of the idle rich can be incredibly boring and it seldom furthers virtues or creativity. Colette's novel "La fin de chérie" (The End of Chérie) gives ample proof of this. Chérie does not kill himself for love, he is far too selfish for such a tragic act. He simply allowed himself to be bored and pampered to the point of no return.

The king of Dur plays chess with the old fakir. The origin of chess goes indeed back to India, around the 6th century AD. From the Far East the game spread to Persia, and after the Arabs took over Persia, to southern Europe. It is a mind game that is related to war and to the patriarchy. The jealousy of Kupti also belongs to the patriarchy. Before the age of patriarchy, the power of women in India was awesome. The ancient ritual of burning a widow together with her dead husband meant long ago that the woman used the power of fire (ram ram) to bring her husband back to life and to rejuvenate both his and her own body. When the true meaning of the ritual was forgotten, widow-burning was reduced to pure sadism and greed: the unwillingness of the family to feed a useless woman.

The monkeys know how to cure the king's dangerous illness brought about by Kupti's poison. Monkeys are sacred in the East, and the Hindu monkey god Hanuman has all the knowledge of herbal medicine. Of course, every living being is sacred, and this would be crystal clear to us if we had a true connection to nature and to our souls and hearts, and if we sometimes slept under a tree like Imani. We might then even understand the language of our animal sisters and brothers. The key to the healing of the poisoned king is exactly that: the understanding of the monkeys' conversation. The animals bestow Imani with all the knowledge she needs: her sister's action, the healing properties of the berries and how to use them.

The two monkeys in the tree say that by living in stuffy houses and stuffy cities we miss knowing all the best things. This is far more true than most people are aware of. The ancient forests that have remained untouched by the greed of men are incredibly rich resources of healing plants. Wild animals know this and can find whatever they need. But we have by now mostly destroyed this paradise. No chemical drug has the intricate sophistication and the wide range of impacts of a plant. We cannot really imitate nature.

The story of Kupti and Imani is free of revenge. There are a great many fairytales that tell us of jealous sisters that will stop at nothing to harm their sibling. Think of Cinderella, The Beauty and the Beast, and many more. Cinderella's sisters are blinded in the end (in the German version, "Aschenputtel"), and the Beauty's sisters turned to stone.

But Imani and her husband are content to let divine justice have its way. Every evil deed sooner or later falls back on the one who commits it. With the berries, Imani is acting as a very competent doctor. This finds a parallel in Shakespeare's "Merchant of Venice", where Portia, disguised as a doctor, saves the life of her husband's best friend. She too asks for a ring that will later prove that she was the one who saved him from a cruel death.

But the most important message of this fairytale is in the beginning. Imani chooses to be her own self as a woman. And so her happy marriage is really a symbol of her marriage with her divine self.

What Came of Picking Flowers

From the Portuguese

There was once a woman who had three daughters whom she loved very much. One day the eldest was walking in a water-meadow, when she saw a pink blossom growing in the stream. She stopped to pick the flower, but her hand had scarcely touched it, when she vanished altogether. The next morning the second sister went out into the meadow, to see if she could find any traces of the lost girl, and as a branch of lovely roses lay trailing across her path, she bent down plucking one of the roses. In a moment she too disappeared. Wondering what could have happened to her two sisters, the youngest followed in their footsteps and fell a victim to a branch of delicious white jessamine. So the old woman was left without any daughter at all.

She wept and wept and wept all day and all night, and went on weeping so long that her late born son, who had been a little boy when his sisters disappeared, grew up to be a tall youth and still she was mourning. Then one night he asked his mother to tell him the cause of her grief. When he had heard the whole story, he said: "Give me your blessing, mother, and I will go and search the world till I find my sisters."

So he set forth and after some time came upon three big boys who were fighting in the road. He stopped and inquired what they were fighting about, and one of them answered: "My lord! Our father left to us, when he died, a pair of boots, a key and a cap. Whoever puts on the boots and wishes himself in any place, he will find himself there. The key will open every door in the world, and with the cap on your head no one can see you. Now our eldest brother wants to have all three things for himself, and we wish to draw lots for them."

"Oh, that is easily settled", said the youth. "I will throw this stone as far as I can, and the one who picks it up first, shall have the three things." So he took the stone and flung it, and while the three brothers were running after it, he took the key and the cap, hastily put on the boots, and said: "Boots, take me to the place where I shall find my eldest sister!"

The next moment the young man was standing on a steep mountain before the gates of a strong castle guarded by bolts and bars and iron chains. The magic key did open the doors of the castle one by one, and he walked through a number of halls and corridors, till he met a beautiful and richly dressed young lady who started back in surprise at the sight of him, and exclaimed: "Oh, sir, how did you get in here?"

The young man replied that he was her brother, and told her by what means he had been able to pass through the doors. In return, she told him how happy she was, except for one thing, and that was, that her husband lay under a spell that could not be broken until there should be put to death a man who could not die.

They talked together for a long time, and then the lady said he had better leave as she expected her husband back at any moment, and he might not like him to be there. But the young man assured her she need not be afraid, as he had with him a cap which would make him invisible. They were still deep in conversation when the door suddenly opened and a bird flew in, but he saw nothing unusual, for, at the first noise, the youth had put on his cap. The lady brought a large golden basin, into which the bird dived, reappearing a moment later as a handsome man. Turning to his wife, he cried: „I am sure someone is in the room!" At this the youth took off his cap and came forward, telling his sister's husband all about his quest. They embraced and the husband gave his brother-in-law a feather and said: "If you are in danger call for me. I am the king of birds and will help you as best as I can."

The youth thanked him and went away. He told the boots to take him to the place where his second sister was living. As before, he found himself at the gates of a huge castle. Within was his second sister, very happy with her husband, who loved her dearly, but longing for the moment when he should be set free from the spell that had kept him half his life a King of Fishes. The youth was given a fish-scale and told to call for the king of fishes if he was in danger.

The young man thanked his brother-in-law and told the magic boots to take him to the place where his youngest sister lived. The boots carried him to a dark cavern, with steps of iron leading down to it. Inside his sister sat weeping and sobbing. When she saw a man standing before her, she cried: "Oh, whoever you are, save me and take me from this horrible place!" When he told her who he was, she related her story. She had been carried off by a monster, who wanted to make her marry him by force, and had kept her a prisoner all these years because she would not submit to his will. Every single day he came to ask her to marry him and to remind her that there was no hope of her being set free, as he would never die. At these words the youth remembered his two enchanted brothers-in-law, and he advised his sister to consent to the monster's plea under the condition that he would tell her why he could never die.

Suddenly everything began to shake as if it was rattled by a whirlwind, and the monster entered. The girl said to him: "I have decided to marry you, if you will tell me why it is that you can never die." The monster laughed and replied: "You are thinking how you would be able to kill me? Well, to do that, you would have to find an iron casket which lies at the bottom of the sea and has a white dove inside, and then you would have to find the egg the dove laid, and bring it here, and dash it against my head." He laughed again and told her: "Now you will be obliged to marry me, as you know my secret." She begged that the wedding might be put off for three days so that she could prepare herself, and the monster consented and went away rejoicing in his victory.

When he had disappeared, the brother took off the cap which had kept him invisible, and told his sister not to lose heart as he hoped in three days she would be free. Then he put on his boots and wished himself to the seashore. And there he was directly. Drawing out the fish-scale, he cried: "Come and help me, King of the Fishes!", and his brother-in-law swam up and asked what he could do. The young man related the story and his brother-in-law asked his subjects to bring the iron casket from the bottom of the sea to the surface. The magic key opened it, and the white dove flew out. The young man called the king of birds and through him the nest of the dove was found and in it lay the egg which was to kill the monster and break the spell and set them all free.

By now it was already far into the third day, which the monster had fixed for the wedding. But the young man returned in time, entered the cavern unseen and dashed the egg straight at the monster's head. It started and with a groan like the rumbling of an earthquake, turned over and died.

To celebrate their freedom, the three girls sent for their mother, whose sorrow was now turned into joy. They had a great feast, and the youngest sister and her brother were rich to the end of their days with the treasures they found in the cave, collected by the monster.

The old woman who is left without any daughter stands for Mother Earth or Demeter, the Greek goddess of fertility. Her three daughters share the fate of Demeter's only child, Persephone, who went out picking flowers and was raped and abducted by Hades, the lord of death. All Demeter could find of Persephone was blood-red poppies scattered over a field. Poppies bleed for mother earth. They grow best where her body has been disturbed and ripped open.

It may be hard for us to imagine this, but there was a time on Earth when nobody would abuse a woman or a child or any other being or element. The entire Earth was held sacred and all her children in the kingdoms of plants, animals and minerals and amongst humans were honoured and loved and cherished.

Earth is a female planet. Therefore once upon a time every woman was revered like her. It was absolutely unthinkable to possess or rape a female. Animals were not hunted or killed. Humans were firmly rooted in the spirit world and needed very little food and were content and happy to eat the fruits, seeds and leaves of trees or bushes.

When Demeter lost her daughter she was so distraught that the earth became a wasteland. In our fairytale the mother is almost transformed into a brook with her endless weeping – like Niobe, the tragic queen of the Greek mythology, whose sons and daughters all died on the same day. That the mother weeps until her son is grown up can be read as symbol of matriarchy giving way to patriarchy.

In the process, many women will have to continue with their bitter sorrow and grieving, until, like now, the earth has truly become a wasteland more and more. That the three young girls disappear from the face of the earth is a metaphor for the fact that in a strictly patriarchal society a woman can sometimes only be in full power of her self if she is dead. We see this very clearly in the famous Ballet stories "La Bayadere" and "Giselle". Both girls must die in order to regain their true selves and be on an equal footing with their male lovers. Drastic measures indeed. In her extended essay "A Room of One's Own" Virginia Woolf wrote that any woman living at the time of Shakespeare, and being equipped with the same genius, could only have done one thing: commit suicide.

But the boy in our fairytale is still the child of the great mother. He misses his sisters and maybe his own female side, his anima, and he sets out to recover what is lost. The magic boots that he finds on his way belong to the ancient gifts of the dreamtime of our planet: the capacity of teleportation. The key to open all doors is a pure heart that asks and knows it will be given what is for the highest good of all that is. It is also the practice of positive visualization. The cap that makes the wearer invisible is a sure sign of mastery. Only those who have mastered their ego issues can be turned invisible. To quarrel over such gifts is obviously the height of stupidity and the three boys show that they are not ready for them. These are treasures that cannot be won by fight or war, and therefore the youth who tricks the boys and takes them is not a thief. He earns them through his pure heart and his intention to use them for an unselfish goal: to find his sisters.

But who is the terrible monster that wants to marry the youngest sister and keeps her a prisoner? This grim bridegroom comes close to Hades, the lord of death, that abducted Demeter's daughter, Persephone. But this monster is also our fear of death, that has indeed grown out of all proportions. Many of today's old people would rather be tortured by new medical inventions than give up the physical body and be free to move on. Some actually want to die, but they cannot bring themselves to let go. To cling to life is to lose the very essence of life: the divine flow. In ancient Egypt "to clutch" signified "to die". In Assyrian "to clutch the mountain" had the same meaning. We still condemn suicide instead of understanding and respecting the fact that the decision to live on Earth or choose another reality is ours to have – unbiased and unconditional, and most certainly untainted by morality.

All three girls are behind lock and key, but the youngest is in a dark cavern and weeps all day long like her mother. If she marries the monster she will have to remain underground for all eternity, because the monster presumably cannot die. That the life force of an ogre is kept in an egg is a motive in many fairytales. Nothing could be more fragile than an egg or more easily broken. But once again we come across a monumental fear of death, as this egg is in an iron casket at the bottom of the sea and still within the dove, that is, as far away and out of reach as possible, because even if the dove were freed she would then fly away never to be found again. That is how we suppress our worst anxieties. The idea to face them, to have the egg finally found and smashed against our heads, seems then not only impossible but ludicrous. And so we live in darkness.

Without the help of the elements Water and Air the hero could never succeed. It is very interesting that the kings of the fishes and of the birds assist the youth in delivering his youngest sister and in doing so break the spell that keeps her in the threedimensional trap. Animals that are out of reach of humans are multidimensional.

But those that have become enslaved by us are caged like we are. The moment we take away the freedom of a living being, we have given up our own freedom. We live in fear and abysmal ignorance. We no longer understand that ALL life is eternal, that we simply change or transform ourselves, but we truly cannot die. Otherwise we would know that the so called "Lord of Death" that steals away our children is not even real. What IS very real is, however, that if we torture and kill hecatombs of animals in order to prolong our own miserable existence, we will experience what agony means and will make ourselves go through all the horrors we want to prevent. We cannot destroy the planet, but we can very easily destroy our own bodies and minds and for a time lose our souls.

Why is the great mother not able to redeem her daughters? I think that in the end phase of matriarchy, the worshipping of the goddess became very dark and cruel in many places on earth. This was partly the reason for the raping, abduction and imprisonment of women. Apart from this we have to face the fact that the ruling of women over men is not better than its opposite. Every kind of imbalance is a time bomb. Right now in our patriarchal societies the abuse of power has become quite blatant. But the young man, who is still a true son of mother earth, is able and willing to redeem his sisters and brother-in-laws and to bring back another golden age of balance and harmony and lasting peace. He is not a bridegroom who enters into a power struggle with his female consort, but simply a brother to all beings, human and otherwise. It is so sad that we call the beings from other planets "aliens" and cannot recognise that they are our brothers and sisters too, and that we are all ONE family in the entire universe and all of creation.

In a great many fairytales it is the sister who frees her brothers. A well known example of this is the German fairytale "The Seven Ravens" by the Grimm brothers. In this tale, the sister travels not only through the entire world to find her seven brothers, she also goes to the sun and to the moon and at last to the morning star, who gives her the key to open the door to the shadow-land. We are all of us called upon to be faithful sisters and brothers to one another, it is the most sacred alliance on earth.

We don't need Antigone to tell us this, we know the truth deep in our hearts. But Antigone, the princess of Thebes, who led her blind father and brother Oedipus (they were both children of the same mother) as a beggar through all of Greece to his final resting place in Athens, she, who was later willing to die in order to give her brother Polynices, who betrayed his country, a decent burial, is a shining example of the true meaning of sisterhood.

Humans, animals and elements work seamlessly together in this fairytale. Something the Earth has not seen in millenia with very few exceptions. If one link in this beautiful chain would have failed, the youngest sister would have to weep forever in her dark prison.

*

From Portugal we now move on to Sicily to hear another version of this old story, from an island that was once a Greek colony.

The Story of Bensurdatu

From Sicily

There was once a king and a queen who had three wonderfully beautiful daughters, and their one thought was how to make their girls happy.

One day the princesses said to the king: "Dear father, we want so much to have a picnic, and eat our dinner in the country!" – "Very well, dear children, let us have a picnic by all means", answered the king.

When luncheon was prepared it was put into a cart, and the royal family stepped into a carriage and drove right away into the country. After a few miles they reached a house and garden belonging to the king, and close by was their favourite place for lunch. The drive had made them hungry, and they ate with a hearty appetite, till almost all the food had disappeared. When they had quite done, the girls said to their parents: "Now we should like to wander about the garden a little, but when you want to go home, just call to us." And they ran off, laughing, down a green glade, which led to the garden.

But no sooner had they stepped across the fence, when a dark cloud came down and covered them, and prevented them seeing wither they were going.

Meanwhile the king and his queen sat lazily among the heather, and an hour or two slipped away. The sun was dropping towards the horizon, and they began to think it was time to go home. So they called to their daughters and called again, but no one answered them. Frightened at the silence, they searched every corner of the garden, the house and the neighbouring wood, but no trace of the girls was to be found anywhere. The earth seemed to have swallowed them up. The poor parents were in despair. The queen wept all the way home and for many days after, and the king issued a proclamation that whoever should bring back his lost daughters should have one of them to wife, and should, after his death, reign in his stead.

Now two young generals were at that time living at the court, and when they heard the king's declaration, they said one to the other: "Let us go in search of them!" And they set out, each mounted on a strong horse.

But although they inquired at every village they came through, they could hear nothing of the princesses, and by-and-by their money was all spent, and they were forced to sell their horses. Even this money lasted only a little while longer and they went to an inn to beg for some food, as they were really starving. They said to the host: "We have no money, please let us stay here and serve you." The innkeeper agreed to this, and the generals remained with him and became his servants.

All this time the king and queen remained in their palace longing for their children, but not a word was heard of them or of the generals who had gone to seek for them.

Now there was living in the palace a faithful servant of the king called Bensurdatu, who had been with him for many years. He said: "Your majesty, let me go and seek your daughters!" – "No, no, Bensurdatu", replied the king, "three daughters have I lost and two generals, and shall I lose you also?" – "Let me go, your majesty; trust me, and I will bring back your daughters."

Then the king gave way, and Bensurdatu set forth, and rode on till he came to the inn, where he dismounted and asked for food. It was brought by the two generals, whom he knew at once. They told him their adventures, and he asked them to join him in his quest.

The three companions rode on for many miles, and at length they came to a wild place, without signs of human beings. It was getting dark and they looked around for a place to sleep. At last they saw a light in the window of a tiny hut.

"Who comes there?" asked a voice, as they knocked at the door. "Oh, have pity on us, and give us a night's shelter!" replied Bensurdatu; we are three tired travellers who have come a long way."

Then the door was opened by a very old woman who stood back and beckoned them to enter. "Whence do you come, and whither do you go?", asked she.

"Ah, good woman, we have a heavy task before us", answered Bensurdatu, „we are bound to find the king's daughters and bring them back to the palace."

"Oh, unhappy creatures!" cried she, "you know not what you are doing! The kings daughters are at the bottom of a deep river, the two eldest are guarded by two giants, and the youngest is watched by a serpent with seven heads."

The generals were filled with terror at her words and wished to return immediately. But Bensurdatu stood firm: "We must carry our quest through. Tell us where the river is." The old woman told them and gave them some cheese, wine and bread, so they should not set forth starving.

The sun had only just risen above the hills next morning before they all woke, and, taking leave of the wise woman who had helped them, they rode on till they came to the river.

"I am the eldest", said one of the generals, "and it is my right to go down first." So the others fastened a cord round him, and gave him a little bell, and let him down into the water. But scarcely had the river closed above his head when such dreadful rushing sounds and peals of thunder came crashing round about him that he lost all his courage, and rang his bell. Great was his relief when the rope began to pull him upwards.

Then the other general plunged in, but he fared no better than the first, and was soon on dry ground again.

"Well, you are a brave pair!" said Bensurdatu, as he tied the rope round his own waist, "let us see what will happen to me." And when he heard the thunder and clamour round about him he thought to himself: "Oh, make as much noise as you like, it won't hurt me!" When his feet touched the bottom he found himself in a large, brilliantly lighted hall, and in the middle sat the eldest princess, and in front of her lay a huge giant, fast asleep. Bensurdatu drew his sword and cut off the giant's head with such a blow that if flew into the corner. The heart of the princess leapt within her, and she placed her golden crown on the head of Bensurdatu, and called him her deliverer.

"Now show me where your sisters are", he said, "that I may free them also."

So the princess opened a door, and led him into another hall, wherein sat her next sister, also guarded by a giant who was asleep and met with the same fate as the first of his kind. The redeemed princess could not find words to thank Bensurdatu enough and she too gave him her golden crown.

"Now show me where your youngest sister is, she who is in the power of the serpent with seven heads. It will be a splendid fight!"

Then the princesses opened a door to a large hall, and there stood the youngest sister, chained fast to the wall, and before her was stretched a serpent with seven heads, horrible to see. As Bensurdatu came forward it twisted all its heads in his direction and made a quick dart to snatch him within its grasp. But Bensurdatu drew his sword and laid about him till the seven heads were rolling on the floor. He then rushed to the princess and broke her chains, and she wept for joy, and embraced him and took the golden crown from her head and gave it to him.

"Now we must go back to the upper world", said Bensurdatu and led her back to her sisters. He tied the rope round the eldest and rung his bell. The generals above heard and drew her gently up. They then threw the rope back in the river and soon the second princess stood beside her sister.

So now there were left only Bensurdatu and the youngest princess. "Dear Bensurdatu", she said, "do me a kindness and let them draw you up before me. I dread the treachery of the generals." – "No", replied Bensurdatu, "I certainly will not leave you down here." – "If it is your wish I will go up; but first I swear that if you do not follow to marry me, I shall stay single for the rest of my life!" Then he bound the rope round her, and the generals drew her up.

But instead of lowering the rope again into the river, envy at the courage and success of Bensurdatu so filled the minds of the two generals, that they turned away and left him to perish. And, more than that, they threatened the princesses and forced them to promise to tell their parents that it was the two generals who had set them free. „And if they should ask about Bensurdatu, you must say that you have never seen him", they added; and the princesses fearing for their lives, promised everything.

The king and the queen were beside themselves with joy when they saw their dear children once more. When the generals had told their lies, the king felt he had to reward them, and that the two elder princesses should become their wives.

And now we must see what Bensurdatu was doing. When the rope never came back he knew that his comrades had betrayed him. He rose and began to search through the three halls, and all of a sudden, he noticed a purse hanging on a wall. He took it down and a voice came from it, saying: "What commands have you?" – "Take me out of this place and into the upper world!" And in a moment he was standing by the river bank.

"Now let me have the most beautiful ship that ever was built!" And there was the ship, with a flag floating from its mast on which were the words, "King with the three crowns." Then Bensurdatu climbed on board and sailed away to the city where the three princesses dwelt.
The king saw the beautiful vessel and said to himself: "That must indeed be a mighty monarch, for he has three crowns while I have only one." He invited him to the castle, thinking: "This will be a fine husband for my youngest daughter!"

"Noble lord", said the king, "let us feast and make merry together, then, if it seems good to you, do me the honour to take my youngest daughter to wife."

Bensurdatu was glad and they all sat down to a great feast. Only the youngest princess was sad, for her thoughts were with Bensurdatu. After they arose from the table, the king said to her: "Dear child, this mighty lord does you the honour to ask your hand in marriage." – "Oh, father", answered she, "spare me, I pray you, for I desire to remain single."

Then Bensurdatu turned to her and said: "If I were Bensurdatu, would you give the same answer to me?" And as she stood silently gazing at him, he added: "Yes, I am Bensurdatu; and this is my story." And he told them what had happened. When he had ended the king stretched out his hand, and said: "Dear Bensurdatu, my youngest daughter shall indeed be your wife; and when I die, my crown shall be yours! As for the men who have betrayed you, they shall leave the country and you shall see them no more."

And the wedding was duly celebrated, and rejoicings were held for three days over the marriage of Bensurdatu and the youngest princess.

In this tale the three girls have not only a mother who weeps for them, but also an astute father who issues a very tempting proclamation in order to regain them.

Patriarchy is well established by now. Before the girls vanish, they step across a fence. The old German word for a witch is Hagazussa, in old Dutch Haghetisse and old English Haegtesse, or in short Hag. In all three languages Hag also means fence or frontier. To step across a frontier is to enter another reality. Zussa means spirit, so this other reality is a spiritual one. Witches were, by their very name, women with outstanding talents who could cross the border between the visible and the spiritual world "beyond".

The princesses are truly in need of help from the other side, for this late version of the ancient tale is already a political one. Intrigue and ambition come into it. Hierarchy is the name of the game. You can go up in this world or down like the two generals who become servants to an innkeeper.

Bensurdatu is also a servant, but he serves the king. If we see the king as heavenly king, Bensurdatu becomes an angel. Human ignorance made the realm of angels into a hierarchy, but this is nonsense. All angels simply serve the light. Christ washed the feet of his disciples and went hand in hand with the felon who was crucified beside him into his kingdom.

Most of his earthly life he was among people who had no social standing of any kind. He clearly did not care for status symbols or for politics. He would not allow himself to be used for an uprising against the Roman empire. His kingdom was a spiritual one where a tiny worm is quite as important as an entire galaxy and All is ONE.

Bensurdatu comes to the inn where the two generals serve food, without delay. He does not march on his stomach like the two generals or like the army of Napoleon, who was likewise a general during the French revolution and as ambitious as they make them. Bensurdatu's needs are few and he knows where he is going. He does not follow the drum but the guidance of his divine self.

The old wise woman who helps him find the princesses is a powerful spiritual guide. She reminds me a bit of Demeter since she knows what nobody could fathom so far. The three girls are deep down in a river. In many cultures a great river is the boundary between life and death. In ancient Greece the river Lethe would take away all thoughts and memories together with the life-force, and all that was left of any being was a mere shadow.

As before in the Portuguese fairytale "What Came of Picking Flowers", we are confronted with the fear of death. But this time the fear does not take the form of a monster, but of two giants and a serpent with seven heads. How apt. The giants show us how overpowering and paralysing this fear can be, and the serpent makes it clear that if you cut off one head there will always be six more to deal with, as she is a symbol for a never ending battle.

However Bensurdatu is not impressed with those theatricals, he can see right through them. He says: "Make as much noise as you like, it won't hurt me!" And he cuts off the giants heads with such a blow, they fly into a corner. That is his way to deal with fear.

Let us tarry a moment here and give the origin of all those stories some thought. Persephone, the first maiden to be snatched away by death as she was picking flowers, could never come back into the land of the living. She remained the wife of Hades, the dark lord of the underworld. So, how is it that in both our fairytales the girls can be brought back to their parents? As we know, a fairytale can span thousands and even hundreds of thousands of years; it can lead us into the far distant future as easily as into the very beginning of time, or both. Both heroes in our two different stories show us visions of things to come. We have invented the fear of death, we fed this fear until it became gigantic and hideous, and so we are without doubt quite able to starve it until it is no more. But how can we do this? We live in a time of growing awareness of angels. The ancient myths and indeed the history of Greece are full with war, with murder, with blood sacrifices, in a word, with death. The ancient Greeks were invaders like the Vikings and left a blood trail behind them when they came down from the north to take over the Greek penninsula. The Greek tragedies teach us to look at our terrible past and to repent and cleanse ourselves, and finally to change our ways of living. This was called "katharsis", meaning "purification and purgation of body and soul through dramatic art that results in renewal and restoration". But in order to turn away from an obsession with death, we need more than katharsis, we need to let go of all ties of religions. All our gods are at least partly cruel, and all are in the final analysis man-made. Of course if we make up gods, we usually give them a certain amount of life energy, so they can become a force to be reckoned with. And there are entities in the astral realm who like to lead us astray by playing god almighty. I can't really blame them, we are such an easy prey; it must be almost irresistibly tempting to fool us. Religions have been used regularly as political controlling tools and are as such mostly fear-based.

Bensurdatu may be an angel, but he is most of all a free spirit. He looks positively forward to fight the serpent with seven heads! He knows that divinity resides within us, not without. We may need law and order, but it is dangerous to claim they come from above. The so called "holy books" have been written by men with ego agendas. Yes, it is possible for human beings to become enlightened. But I am very sure that those who reach that level do not feel tempted, inclined or urged to lay down the laws for other beings. They want others to be free, and know that the cosmic laws that are within us, like our souls, and not written in stone.

The giants and the serpent that guard the princesses are not only symbols for the fear of death, they are excellent substitutes for the religious laws that keep women "chained fast to the wall", like the youngest daughter. To be force-married as a child nine years of age, to be mutilated or killed for desiring a life (and love) of one's own choice, is every bit as bad as a hideous serpent with seven heads! Our three girls may be snatched away from the giants and from the serpent by Bensurdatu, but they are not yet out of the wood. Now they are in the power of the generals, and Bensurdatu is left at the bottom of the river.

In many fairytales humans are able to live under water. They find there another realm that shamans call "the lower world". It can be in a river, in a lake or ocean or simply underground. After his fight with the serpent Bensurdatu says: "Now we must go back to the upper world!" But although he manages to send the girls up, he himself is forced to stay on to make another experience on his path of spiritual development.

The "magic purse" that Bensurdatu finds in the lower world is our connection to the miraculous. Many wonderful and extremely helpful things can be found on a shamanistic journey. As I said before, if we are willing to become aware of the miracles in our lives, everything changes for the better. We then see not only our own world but the entire universe as miraculous. The purse asks: "What commands have you?" If we want our wishes to come true, we have to be totally clear what we want (and also what is truly the best for us and for all around us). Then we have to send out our commands in a positive way to the universe with the firm belief and indeed with the knowledge that we are being heard and answered. Negative wishes cannot be received by higher powers, because for them negativity does not exist. In higher dimensions there is no darkness, only eternal light.

The oath of the youngest princess to stay single if Bensurdatu does not follow her is very significant! Sometimes the only road to freedom is to stay alone. That all three girls are willing to leave the man who rescued them to his almost certain death, is a clear indication that freedom cannot be given to us, we must also want it with all our hearts and be ready to do our bit to hold on to it. Bensurdatu did not hesitate to risk his life for the princesses. But they are afraid to do the same for him. The girls are deeply traumatized and need healing first to become strong and independent. But instead two of them get married to traitors and are forced to live a life of lies.

For the king and the queen the happiness of their children is important. The same cannot be said for their husbands. This is the trouble with politics and intrigue. The proclamation of the king does not so much draw people who sincerely wish to be helpful, but those that are ambitious and determined to do better for themselves no matter how.

If we compare the two fairytales we notice that in the first version the girls disappear simply by picking flowers. A bit naive, and, as far as storytelling and myths go, not very convincing. In the second version a dark cloud envelops the paradise garden where the children play together: the dark ages. Again and again every country in the entire world has been overshadowed by cruel invaders who smashed peaceful and sometimes very refined cultures and enslaved or killed the population until there was nothing left but invaders and their creed of violence. We are all children of invaders. Our way to freedom and mastery therefore cannot be our DNA – it must be found within our past and future selves. We all lived in the paradise state once. We must remember, activate and manifest this NOW.

In the Portuguese version the two elder girls are married to powerful kings with good intentions. In Sicily however, the lower world becomes more or less a symbol for hell. In the middle ages, due to the Roman Catholic faith (which still reigns supremely in the south of Italy) shamanism was condemned as devil worship. And so all three princesses are doomed, but in both versions the youngest is singled out for the worst possible fate. She is, like Persephone, the Kore, the maiden: one of the oldest images on earth of the Shekina, the female soul of creation. As we know, the Shekina had to go into exile. Everywhere. We are awaiting her return even more eagerly than the return of Christ, whether we are aware of this or not. The entire planet awaits her return. Her marriage is a vision of the future. Just like the coming back to life of the dead queen Hermione and the return of her lost daughter in the last act of Shakespeare's wonderful "Winter's Tale".

Naturally the Shekina, like the Christ consciousness, must return within ourselves, not without. As we clearly saw in the fairytales, we cannot become entirely free through the deeds of others, but ultimately only through our own clear intentions and actions. We all have a female side, women AND men alike. Bensurdatu is given his three golden crowns by the three maidens as a confirmation of his female aspect. At the same time it is very important for the three maidens to free themselves of their victim-consciousness, to discover their male sides and stand up for their independence.

Why did it have to be the only daughter of Demeter, Persephone, that was raped and abducted and killed (that is, brought to the land of shadows)? Of all the many goddesses, why her? Demeter is the great mother. Without her blessing nothing can live and grow on earth. Before ancient Greece was invaded, she was omni-potent. Like Allah she had no consort. She was the one, the sole, the supreme. How can you best destroy a mother? By attacking, harming and murdering her children.

There is another myth in ancient Greece (beside that of Demeter and Persephone) that has an echo in this fairytale: the story of Andromeda. Like the youngest princess, Andromeda was chained to a rock and threatened by a dragon. She was the daughter of the Ethiopian king Cepheus and of his wife Cassiopeia. All three can be seen in the night sky as star constellations. Andromeda was rescued and married by Perseus and their descendants ruled Mycenai in the Peloponnese before Atreus, the son of Pelops, grandson of Tantalus and father of Agamemnon, the destroyer of Troy, took over. As we can see, there is no balance here between male and female. Andromeda did make no attempt to master her fate. Her husband Perseus, who cut off the head of Medusa (who was probably an Amazon queen in Libya in North-Africa) is a rather grim example of a Greek patriarch. His connection to Pegasos, the winged horse of the muses, is, in my opinion, male propoganda, wishful thinking and the usual white-washing of a very ugly reality. And yet, the name Andromeda is most certainly one of power. The magnificent Andromeda galaxy contains one trillion stars and is double the size of our own Milky Way galaxy. The Persian astronomer Abd al-Rahman al-Sufi discovered her in 964, and by now everyone who has a telescope can admire her radiant beauty. The Greeks could not grasp the concept of a powerful woman. Each and every one of them that came within their radius got either a very bad press (like Medusa or Medea) or was made into a goddess (like Artemis and Pallas Athene, both clearly inspired by Amazons).

Of course the image of a helpless maiden threatened by a dragon is not confined to Greek mythology, it is all over the place. The patron saint of Great Britain, St. George, for instance rushed to rescue such a virgin in distress. But as Carl Gustav Jung did point out, the virgin in question had actually a lovely understanding with her dragon companion, she was not at all in danger. I would go one step further and say that the dragon could very well be a living symbol for the power of the female.

The Story of Prince Ahmed and the Fairy Paribanou

Arabian Nights

There was a sultan, who had three sons and a niece. The eldest of the princes was called Houssain, the second Ali, the youngest Ahmed, and the princess, his niece, Nouronnihar.

The princess Nouronnihar was the daughter of the younger brother of the sultan, who had died and left the princess very young. The sultan took upon himself the care of his niece's education, and brought her up in his palace with the three princes, planning to marry her off when she arrived at a proper age, and to contract an alliance with some neighbouring prince by that means. But when he perceived that the three princes, his sons, loved her passionately, he thought more seriously about that affair. He was very much concerned. The difficulty he foresaw was to make them agree, and that the two younger ones should consent to yield her up to their elder brother. As he found them positively obstinate, he sent for them all together, and said to them: "I think it would not be amiss if every one of you travelled into a different country. I promise my niece in marriage to him that shall bring me the most extraordinary rarity. I will give you every one a sum of money."

That very day the three princes took their leave of the sultan and set out, each dressed as a merchant. They went the first day's journey together, and passed the night all at an inn. In the morning they agreed to go each their own way for a year and to meet again at the inn.

Prince Houssain, the eldest, went to Bisnagar, the capital of the kingdom of that name. There was a multitude of shops there, stocked with all sorts of merchandise. There were the finest linens from several parts of India, some painted in the most lively colours, and representing beasts, trees and flowers. There were silks and brocades from Persia and porcelain from China. Prince Houssain admired the great number of rose-sellers who crowded the streets; for the Indians are great lovers of that flower.

One morning he saw a crier pass by with a piece of tapestry on his arm and called to him. When he had examined the tapestry that could be bought for thirty purses he told the crier that he could not comprehend why the price for it was set so high.

The crier replied: "I have orders to raise the price to forty purses, and not to part with it under." – "Certainly", answered Prince Houssain, "it must have something extraordinary in it of which I know nothing of." – "You are right, sir. Whoever sits on this piece of tapestry may be transported in an instant to wherever he desires to be." The crier convinced the prince of the truth by transporting both of them to the prince's apartment. Here the crier received forty pieces of gold and prince Houssain became the possessor of the wonderful flying carpet.

Prince Ali, the second son, traveled to Schiraz, the capital of the kingdom of Persia. Among all the criers who passed back and forth with all sorts of goods, he was surprised to see one who held an ivory telescope in his hand and cried it at thirty purses. He asked the man what special virtue the telescope had and was told that by looking into it, he would be able to see whatever object he wished to behold. The prince, wishing to see his father, looked into the telescope and he immediately beheld the sultan in perfect health, set on his throne, in the midst of his council. Afterwards he longed to see the princess Nouronnihar and saw her presently at her toilet table laughing, in a pleasant humour, with her women about her. He gave the crier his money and received the magic glass.

Prince Ahmed, the youngest, took the road to Samarkand. Here one of the criers had an apple in his hand and wanted five and thirty purses for it. He claimed that it could cure all sickness. Even if a man was already at the point of death, the apple would restore him to perfect health just through its wonderful perfume. A great many persons confirmed what the crier said and prince Ahmed was very glad to buy it there and then.

After one year the three princes met again at the inn and showed each other their treasures. Immediately they saw through the glass that the princess Nouronnihar was dying. They then sat down on the carpet, wished themselves with her, and were there in a moment. Prince Ahmed put the apple under Nouronnihars nose, and she rose up in her bed, and asked to be dressed, just as if she had woken up of a sound sleep. Her women informed her that she was obliged to the three princes for the sudden recovery of her health, and she expressed her joy and gratitude to them.

Later the three princes went to throw themselves at their father's feet, and pay their respect to him. The sultan embraced them with the greatest joy, both for their return and for the recovery of the princess, who had been given up by the physicians. Now the princes presented each his rarity. The sultan remained some time silent. Then he said: "I would declare for one of you children with a great deal of pleasure if I could do it with justice. But the only fruit you have reaped from your travels is the glory of having equally contributed to restore the health of the princess, your cousin. So go and get each of you a bow and arrow, and repair to the great plain. I'll soon come to you, and I will give the princess Nouronnihar to him that shoots the farthest."

The sultan appeared and prince Houssain took his bow and arrow and shot first. Prince Ali shot next and much beyond him. Prince Ahmed had a go, but nobody could see where his arrow fell; and though it was believed that he may have shot the farthest, it was necessary that his arrow should be found. So the sultan judged in favour of Prince Ali, and gave orders for preparations to be made for the wedding.

Prince Houssain would not honour the feast with his presence. He left the court and became a hermit.

Prince Ahmed, too, did not come to the wedding. He resolved to search for his arrow. He went to the place where prince Ali's arrow had been found and straight forward from there. He walked on and on until he came to some steep craggy rocks where at long last he perceived his arrow. "Certainly", he said to himself, "no man living could shoot an arrow so far. There must be some mystery in this. Perhaps fortune, to make amends for depriving me of what I thought the greatest happiness, may have reserved a greater blessing for my comfort."

As these rocks were full of caves, the prince entered into one and saw an iron door. Thrusting against it, it opened, and he discovered an easy descent. At first he thought he was going into the dark, but presently a quite different light succeeded that which he came out of, and he perceived a magnificent palace. At the same time a lady of majestic port and air advanced towards him and said: "Come nearer, Prince Ahmed, you are welcome!"

It was no small surprise to the prince to hear himself named in a place he had never heard of. He kneeled before the lady and, rising up again, he said to her: "Madam, I return you a thousand thanks for your assurance of a welcome to a place where I believed my imprudent curiosity had made me penetrate too far. Dare I ask how you know me?" – "Prince, let us go into the hall, there I will answer your question."

The lady led prince Ahmed into a hall and sat down on a sofa and bade him to do the same. She said: "You are undoubtedly sensible that your religion teaches you that the world is inhabited by genies as well as men. I am one of those and my name is Paribanu. I was present when you drew your arrow, and foresaw it would not go beyond Prince Houssains. I took it in the air and gave it the necessary motion to strike against the rocks near where you found it, and I tell you that it lies in your power to make use of the favorable opportunity which presents itself to make you happy."

As the beautiful Fairy looked tenderly upon prince Ahmed with a modest blush on her cheeks, it was no hard matter for the prince to comprehend what happiness she meant. "Madam", he replied, "should I all my life have the good fortune to be your slave, and the admirer of the many charms which ravish my soul, I should think myself the most blessed of man!"

"Prince", said the Fairy, "will you not pledge your faith to me?" – "Yes, my lady", answered the prince in an ecstasy of joy, "yes, my queen, I will give you my heart without the least reserve!" The wedding feast was celebrated the next day, and all the days following were a continual feast.

At the end of six months the prince desired to know how his father was and asked the Fairy to give him leave to visit his court.

"Prince", she said, "go when you please. But don't take it amiss if I give you some advice. I don't think it wise to tell the sultan of our marriage, nor of my quality. Beg of him to be satisfied in knowing you are happy." The Fairy gave him a horse, which was finely caparisoned, and was as

beautiful a creature as any in the sultan's stable.
The prince bid her adieu and set forward on his journey.
The sultan received his youngest son with great joy.
The prince told a story of his adventures without speaking
of the fairy, and ended: "The only favor I ask of your
majesty is to give me leave to come often and pay you
my respects, and to know how you do." Prince Ahmed
stayed for three days at the sultan his father's court, and
the fourth he returned to the Fairy Paribanu.

A month after prince Ahmed's return the Fairy observed
that the prince never talked of his father, as if there had
been no such person in the world. Therefore she asked him:
"Prince, have you forgotten the sultan, your father? Don't
you remember the promise you made to go and see him
often?" So the prince went next morning, and for several
months he did visit his father often, always in a richer and
finer equipage.

At last some vizir made the sultan jealous of his son,
saying it was to be feared he might inveigle himself into
the people's favor and dethrone him. The sultan sent for
a female magician and said to her: "Follow my son, and
watch him so well as to find out where he retires and bring
me word."

The magician went to the place where prince Ahmed had
found his arrow, and when the prince appeared she faked
a violent illness, and in this manner she was brought into
the hidden palace of the Fairy. Paribanu ordered two
of her women to take care of her and said to the prince:
"This woman is not so sick as she pretends to be. She is an
imposter who will be the cause of great trouble to you.
But I will deliver you out of all the snares that shall be
laid for you."

A day later the magician went back to the sultan and told
him how very rich prince Ahmed was since his marriage
with the Fairy, richer than all the kings in the world.

Now the vizir advised that the prince should be killed,
but the magician said: "Make him give you all kinds of
wonderful things, by the Fairy's help, till she tires of him
and sends him away."

First the sultan asked his son for a pavillion which might
be carried in a mans hand, and which should be so large as
to shelter his whole army. After he got it, he wanted some
water from the Fountain of Lions, a sovereign remedy
against all sickness. Having received this, he made a re-
quest to meet a man not above a foot and a half high, who
should carry a bar of iron upon his shoulder of five hun-
dredweight. Prince Ahmed, who did not believe that there
was such a man as his father described, would gladly have
excused himself, but the sultan persisted in his demand.

When the prince returned to his beloved Paribanu, she
laughed and said: "There is no difficulty in finding this
man, he is my brother Schaibar. He is of so violent a
nature that nothing can prevent his giving cruel marks
of his resentment for any offence. I will send for him, but
be sure to prepare yourself against being frightened at
his extraordinary figure when you see him." – "What, my
queen", replied prince Ahmed, "do you say Schaibar is

your brother? Let him be ever so ugly or deformed, I shall be so far from being frightened at the sight of him that, as your brother, I shall honour and love him!"

Schaibar soon appeared before them, and the Fairy introduced her husband and said: "The sultan, his father, wishes to see you, and I desire he may be your guide to the sultan's court." When they arrived, Schaibar went boldly and fiercely up to the throne and accosted the sultan in this words: "Thou hast asked for me. See, here I am. What wouldst thou have with me?"

The sultan, instead of answering him, clapped his hands before his eyes to avoid the sight of so terrible an object; at which uncivil and rude reception Schaibar was so much provoked that he instantly lifted up his iron bar and killed him then and there and his vizir with him. He then asked that a certain female magician be brought before him. As soon as she appeared, he said: "Take the reward for thy pernicious counsel, and learn to feign sickness again!" and hit her with his iron bar. He then led the prince back to the Fairy's realm. Prince Ahmed and the Fairy Paribanu remained in seclusion, and they lived happily ever after.

"Pari" and "banu" are two Persian words with the same meaning: fairy or female spirit.

The name of the beautiful princess, Nouronnihar (Nurunnihar) signifies "Light of the Day". Of course the three princes did not care to live without sunlight, and it is no wonder they loved her so much. Still, in spite of her wonderful name, the princess is, like all women in a confirmed patriarchy, merely a commodity to contract an alliance with or otherwise to be handed over to the winner of the game like a trophy. To ask Nouronnihar if she could love the one or the other of the princes is a thought that would not have entered the sultan's mind in the darkest or in the most enlightened of his dreams.

The famous stories from "One Thousand and One Nights" collected in Arabic during the Islamic Golden Age (around 1500 AD) are often referred to in English as "Arabian Nights". The tales compiled over centuries by different authors trace their roots back to ancient Arabic, Indian, Persian and Mesopotamic folklore and literature. They were a major influence in literature. The massive French collection "Le Cabinet des Fées" (17th and 18th century, the salon era of fairytales) was certainly inspired by it, maybe even partly an imitation. The popular versions of "Cinderella" and "The Sleeping Beauty" transform the mother of Cinderella into a fairy godmother, and the wise women at the Sleeping Beauty's christening are by now also largely known as fairies. The Viennese writer Ferdinand Raimund got his Persian fairy Cheristane in his original musical "Der Verschwender" (1834, Theater in der Josephstadt) straight out of "One Thousand and One Nights".

The frame story of "Arabian Nights", the near tragedy of Scheherazade and the very real tragedy of her predecessors has many parallels in African fairytales. The message thereof, that all women are by nature flagrantly lewd and cannot be trusted at all and it is best to kill them after you have had sex with them, because even if you imprison them in the harshest possible way they will find a way to be unfaithful, this message and belief led to all kinds of terrible measures beside the killings. Men who guarded a harem were castrated, and women all over Africa are even today still mutilated in the most cruel fashion, making puberty, marriage and motherhood and just being female a never ending martyrdom.

I think it is impossible to fathom this peculiar misunderstanding of the female nature. The mere wish to control and enslave women cannot answer for the horrible consequences of this completely absurd belief that even if you keep a woman in a box that is closed tight with four bolts of steel to which you have the only four keys she will still find a hundred lovers to betray you. Celtic women in England and Ireland were free to choose their lovers and it was perfectly natural for them to favour first one and then another man. I hope, dear readers, that if we find freedom and choice in matters of the heart acceptable, we also grant it to both sexes, women as well as men. In some areas of archaic Greece and Africa, however, the roles were reversed: queens took a new bridegroom every year and killed the old one. It was considered bad luck if the young king died before his year was up.

The myth of Adonis, who got killed by a wild boar, goes back to this abominable custom. We cannot blame men for wanting this tradition stopped. What we should critize is that they merely reversed the roles, enslaving their enslavers in turn. The redeeming insight "Do not unto others what you wouldn't have them do unto you" had not been written yet. However, even today, two thousand years after it's been written, it is a fact that men can be very much afraid of women and, as we can see, not without reason.

Back to the story. The lovely Scheherazade is forced to tell a new tale every night for more than three years to bargain for her life. Each day could be her last on earth. She knows king Scheherban has already murdered his wife, all his female slaves and all the daughters of his nobles. He made his vizier kill his wife (Scheherazade's mother), and in his realm only two young women are still alive, Scheherazade and her sister Dinarsad. This king does indeed fear women, the mere thought they could call their souls their own makes him tremble in his shoes. He does not realize that to make love with one's body is sometimes not half as real as making love in one's mind, one's thoughts and one's spirit, and that every imprisoned being naturally dreams of real feelings and independence. In plain words: the king is stupid. And that is exactly why he has every reason to be afraid. Is there a cure for such an extreme tunnel vision? King Scheherban is a proud monarch, and pride is just another word for stupidity and single-mindedness. It keeps him isolated and unable to learn and progress.

In a cosmic consciousness we are ONE with all creation and with our divine self, there are no kings, no slaves and no favourites, no-one is chosen and no-one rejected.

In most fairytales it is not a king who kills all young women, it is a monster out of the deep. Finally, when only the kings beloved daughter is left to be sacrificed to the terrible creature, the hero appears and kills it. In the frame story of the "Arabian Nights" there is no such hero. Scheherazade rescues herself and her sister. But the curious resemblance between king Scheherban and the monster is telling. A free and powerful woman is foreign to the king's mind. In the end he does not kill Scheherazade, but she is not free either, she lives because she pleases him. Maybe her stories have a subtle influence on him. But we must not forget that they are told to entertain a tyrant and to prolong a death sentence.

Let us move on to the three princes who compete for the hand of Nouronnihar, the light of the day. The eldest, prince Houssain, travels to Bisnagar, which was once a very large kingdom in Asia comprising the realms of Kanara, Messowr, Travankor, Madura, Marava and Tanjour. Some of the authors of "Arabian Nights" had little understanding of history or geography. One of them describes China as an island under the rule of a Persian king. We are told that Indians love the rose above all other flowers. But it is actually Persia where the rose was specially cultivated and revered as an all-healing remedy. From there it was brought to Europe. In India the state flowers are predominantly lotus, marigold, orchids and rhododendron. But ancient Persia was for a very long time one of the main powers in Western and Eastern Asia. The Sasanian empire encompassed at one time all of Iran, Iraq, Eastern Arabia, the Levant, the Caucasus, Egypt, parts of Turkey, Yemen and Pakistan. Its cultural influence did indeed reach all the way to China and also to Western Europe. The "Arabian Nights" owe much to the first and the second Persian empire.

Prince Houssain obtains a flying carpet, prince Ali a magic telescope, and the youngest, prince Ahmed, who took the silk road to Samarkand, finds an apple from the tree of life. Again we encounter here gifts from the dreamtime of earth. At first all those gifts resided within us. In the present day and age they have become objects that can be bought. We have gone down this road now for a very long time. Our flying carpets are airplanes. Instead of a clear vision we have television, and alas, we have exchanged the healing and rejuvenating apple of Eve, Freya and Harmonia for pharmaceuticals.

The three princes work beautifully together to heal their cousin, they act like one being. But then the sultan orders a competition and the unity is lost. One of humanity's greatest obstacles is our sense of separation. But the universe is really an infinite interconnectivity and in this we have access to all knowledge, all love and all things possible and impossible.

Prince Ahmed is an inspired young man. When he follows his seemingly vanished arrow, he is faced with a mystery. But he is soon wise enough to realize that what he imagined to be a great loss is in fact a great blessing. So often when a marriage comes to an end or when we are fired from a job, we assume this is the end of the world, when in actual fact, it could be the beginning of something new and wonderful.

Enter the Fairy Paribanu. Here we have at long last a woman of power. One that is not afraid to propose to a man. The tale says: "Presently a quite different light succeeded that which he (prince Ahmed) came out of." This is the beautiful light of another world, another reality. A quantum leap in human consciousness is mostly prevented by our ego agendas. The ego wants to be "safe" and to stay inside the three-dimensional box. Most of all it wants to control us. It also wants comfort, whether this is for the highest good for all that is, or not. It worries what others might think or do to us. It wants to be accepted and admired at all cost.

Prince Ahmed does not consult his ego. He marries the Fairy and gives her his heart without the least reserve. The illusions of the material reality mean nothing to him from now on, and he could easily forget his father and all his human connections, but he made a promise, and the Fairy wants him to honour this. Unfortunately, his father's vizir soon becomes jealous, and the sultan himself becomes a victim of his own greed. Why the sultan should want the healing waters from the Fountain of Lions when his son has already brought him an apple that can cure any illness, has to remain a mystery. The monster he is so curious to see is of his own making. Greed is one of the worst human vices and always destroys those that invite it in.

I have considerably shortened this fairytale because I don't think it is necessary to say the same thing three or four times, and I have changed the ending of it. That a Fairy should want to be sultaness of the Indies is not only highly unlikely, it is absurd. There was only once a pope in Rome that was a saint, and he was buried alive. The legend has it that Christ was tempted by Satan to kneel before him and so become emperor of all the world. I am quite certain that Christ never even considered such a thing. Neither would Paribanu.

The Magic Kettle

A Japanese Fairytale

Right in the middle of Japan, high up among the mountains, an old man lived in his little house. He was very proud of it, and never tired of admiring the whiteness of his straw mats, and the pretty papered walls, which in warm weather he always slid back, so that the smell of the trees and the flowers might come in.

One day he was standing looking at the mountain opposite when he heard a kind of rumbling noise in the room behind him. He turned round, and in the corner he beheld a rusty old iron kettle, which could not have seen the light of day for many years. How the kettle got there the old man did not know, but he took it up and looked it over carefully, and when he found that it was quite whole, he cleaned the dust off and carried it into his kitchen.

"That was a piece of luck", he said, smiling to himself, "a good kettle costs money, and it is as well to have a second one at hand in case of need, mine is getting worn out, and the water is already beginning to come through its bottom."

Then he took the older one off the fire, filled the new one with water, and put it in its place. No sooner was the water in the kettle getting warm than such a strange thing happened that the man thought he must be dreaming. First the handle of the kettle gradually changed its shape and became a head, and the spout grew into a tail, while out of the body sprung four paws, and in a few minutes the man found himself watching not a kettle, but a tanuki! The creature jumped off the fire and bounded about the room like a kitten, running up the walls and over the ceiling, till the old man was in an agony lest his pretty room should be spoilt. He cried to a neighbour for help, and between them they managed to catch the tanuki, and shut him up safely in a wooden chest. Then, quite exhausted, they sat down on the mats and consulted together what they should do with this troublesome beast. At length they decided to sell it and bade a passing child to send them a certain tradesman called Jimmu.

When Jimmu arrived, the old man lifted the lid of the wooden chest, but to his surprise, no tanuki was there, nothing but the kettle he had found in a corner. It was very odd, but the man remembered what had taken place on the fire, so after a little bargaining about the price, Jimmu went away carrying the kettle with him.

Jimmu had not gone very far before he felt that the kettle was getting heavier and heavier, and by the time he reached home he was so tired that he was thankful to put it down in the corner of his room. In the middle of the night he was awakened by a loud noise in the corner where the kettle stood. He jumped up and saw that the kettle had become a tanuki, which was running round after his own tail.

The tradesman sighed and went back to sleep, and when he woke up again, there was no tanuki, only an old kettle.

In the morning Jimmu set off to tell his story to a friend next door. The man listened quietly. In his youth he had heard something of a wonder-working kettle. He said: "Go and travel with it and show it off, and you will become a rich man. But be careful to first ask the tanuki's permission!"

Jimmu thanked his friend for his counsel which he followed exactly. The tanuki's consent was obtained, a booth was built, and a notice was hung up outside, inviting people to come and witness the most wonderful transformation that was ever seen. Spectators came in crowds, and the kettle was passed from hand to hand, and they were allowed to examine it all over and to look inside. Then Jimmu took it back and set it on a platform and commanded it to become a tanuki.

"Dance!" said Jimmu, and the tanuki did his steps and moved first to one side and then to the other, till the people could not stand still any longer, and began to dance, too. Gracefully he led the fan-dance, and glided without a pause into the shadow-dance and the umbrella-dance, and it seemed as if he might go on dancing for ever. And so very likely he would have, if Jimmu had not declared he had danced enough and it was time for the booth to be closed.

Jimmu became a rich man, and since he was also an honest one, he put a hundred gold pieces into the kettle and gave it back to the seller and said: "I have no right to keep it any longer, so I give it back to you and a hundred gold pieces as the price for its hire."

The old man thanked Jimmu, and said few people would have been as honest as he. Everything went well with them till they died.

A tanuki is a Japanese racoon dog, a subspecies of the Asian racoon dog. This pretty animal has been significant in Japanese folklore since ancient times. It is a master of disguise and shapeshifting. Japan is one of the few countries on earth with a continuous tradition of shamanism since the world was young.

In spite of that, nobody in this funny little story wishes to penetrate the surprising event that an old kettle becomes a tanuki. The old man simply wants to sell the animal because his pretty little house could suffer. The tradesman uses the magic kettle as a show attraction to make money. At least he asks the tanuki's consent in the matter. And he is honest enough to share his profit with the old man. But is money really all that matters to us? Do we have to sell out spirituality and finally our souls and hearts?

Is this transformation truly "the most wonderful that was ever seen"? Of course not. But the illusionist has replaced the magician, and most people do no longer understand the difference between the two. I would like to quote the author Patricia McKillip (The Book of Atrix Wolfe): "... the great mage (magician) moves from moment to moment, from shape to shape, to meet the constant, everchanging needs of life. From stone, to eagle, to healer, when stillness, flight, life are required, those mages of greatest power must involve themselves in a continuing flow of power, for power unused, power neglected or refused, will find its own shape, its own destructive path in the world. Each moment must concern itself with life, for the renegade mage who chooses to deal in death, will wear the face of death, and in the end, become the motionless, powerless shape of death ..."

If money is too important to us, we lose the matrix of divine flow, we neglect our powers and we become addicted to death (as indeed our society is).

It is quite nice that the tanuki dances and inspires his audience to dance with him. But there is just a slight hint of circus and "dance, little gigolo, dance!" in his performance. The tanuki is no geisha, is he? With all due respect for this ancient and rightfully revered profession.

What would you do if an old teapot appeared before you out of nowhere and later transfomed into a lovely and lively little animal?

I would ask the tanuki why it had come to me and why it chose to be a teapot, in other words, I would ask it to be my teacher.

The Enchanted Pig

A Rumanian Fairytale

Once upon a time there lived a king who had three daughters. Now it happened that he had to go out to battle, so he called his daughters and said to them: "My dear children, I am obliged to go to the wars. The enemy is approaching us with a large army. It is a great grief to me to leave you all. During my absence take care of yourselves and look after everything in the house. You may walk in the garden and go into all the rooms in the palace, except the room in the back in the right-hand corner. Into that you must not enter, for harm would befall you."

His daughters kissed his hands with tears in their eyes and wished him prosperity, and he gave the eldest the keys. The girls decided to work for part of the day, to read for part of the day, and to enjoy themselves in the garden for part of the day. As long as they did this, all went well with them. But this happy state of things did not last long. Every day they grew more and more curious, until the eldest princess said: "Why should we not go into the room that our father forbade us to enter?"

"Sister", said the youngest, "how can you tempt us to break our father's command?" – "Surely the sky will not fall about our heads if we do go in!" said the second princess. While they were speaking thus, they had reached the room. The eldest fitted the key into the lock, and, snap, the door stood open.

The three girls entered and saw a large table with a gorgeous cloth, and on it lay a big open book. The eldest princess stepped up to it and read: "The eldest daughter of this king shall marry a prince from the East." The second girl turned over the page and read: "The second daughter of this king will marry a prince from the West."

Both girls were delighted, but the youngest princess did not want to go near the table. Her elder sisters however left her no peace, and dragged her up to the book, where in fear and trembling she read: "The youngest daughter of this king will marry a pig from the north." If a thunderbolt had fallen from heaven it would not have frightened her more. Her sisters tried to comfort her, saying: "How can you believe such nonsense?"

In the meantime, the king had won a great victory and he hurried home to his daughters. He was happy to see that they were all well, but it was not long before he noticed that his third daughter was getting very thin and sad-looking. It flashed through his mind that the princesses might have disobeyed his word. He called all three girls to him and ordered them to speak the truth. They confessed everything, and the king was so distressed that he was almost overcome by grief. But he saw that what had happened had happened, and that a thousand words would not alter matters by a hair's breadth.

One fine day a prince from the East appeared and asked the king for the hand of his eldest daughter. The king gladly gave his consent and a great wedding feast was celebrated.

After some time the same thing befell the second daughter wo was wooed and won by a prince from the East.

Again time passed, until low and behold! One fine day an enormous pig from the north walked into the palace, and going straight up to the king said: "Hail, oh king! May your life be as prosperous and bright as a sunrise on a clear day!" – "I am glad to see you well, friend", answered the king, "but what wind has brought you hither?" – "I come a-wooing", replied the pig.

Now the king was astonished to hear so fine a speech from a pig, and at once it occured to him that something strange was the matter. He sent for his daughter and advised her to submit to fate, saying: "My child, the words and the whole behaviour of this pig are courteous. Depend upon it some magic or witchcraft has been at work. Marry him and I feel sure that heaven will shortly send you release." – "If you wish me to do this, dear father, I will do it", replied the princess.

After the wedding the pig and his bride set out for his home. When they reached it, they had supper together and went to bed. At night the princess woke up and noticed that the pig had changed into a man. She remembered her father's words and took courage. Night after night the pig became a man and every morning he was changed back into a pig. Clearly, he must be bewitched, the princess thought. In time she grew fond of her husband, he was so kind and gentle.

One fine day she saw an old woman go past. She felt quite excited, as it was long since she had seen a human being, and she called to the woman to come and talk to her. Among other things the hag told her that she understood magic arts, and the princess asked her what could be the matter with her husband.

"Here, my dear child", said the witch, "take this thread, but do not let him know about it, for if he did, it would lose its healing power. At night, when he is asleep, you must get up very quietly and fasten the thread round his left foot as firmly as possible. Do this and you will see in the morning he will not change back into a pig."

The princess did as she was told, but as she was pulling the knot tight there was a crack, and the thread broke, for it was rotten. Her husband awoke with a start and said to her: "Unhappy woman, what have you done? Three days more and this unholy spell would have fallen from me. But now I must go at once, and we shall not meet again until you have worn out three pairs of iron shoes and blunted a steel staff in your search of me." So saying he disappeared.

When the princess was left alone she began to weep and moan in a way that was pitiful to hear. But when she saw that her tears did her no good, she got up, determined to find her husband. She ordered three pairs of iron sandals and a steel staff, and set out. On and on she wandered over nine seas and across nine continents, and she never looked back. At last, worn out and overcome with sorrow, she reached the house of the Moon. The princess knocked at the door and the mother of the Moon, when she saw her sad plight, felt compassion for her, and took her in and nursed and tended her. And while she was here, the princess had a little baby. When it was time for her to part, she said: "I shall always be thankful to you, but can I ask you one last favour? Can your daughter, the Moon, tell me where my husband is?" – "She cannot tell you that, my child. But if you will travel towards the East until you reach the dwelling of the Sun, he may be able to tell you something." Then she gave the princess a roast chicken to eat, and warned her to be very careful not to lose any of the bones, because they might be of great use to her.

The princess had worn out one pair of shoes, and had put on a second pair. She tied the chicken bones into a bundle, and taking her baby into her arms and her staff in her hand, she set out once more on her wanderings.

On and on and on she went across bare sandy deserts, where the roads were so heavy that for every two steps she took forward, she fell back one. Next she crossed swamps and high rocky mountains until at length, wearied to death, she reached the house of the Sun. She knocked and begged for admission. The mother of the Sun opened the door and wept with pity when she heard all the princess had suffered. She promised to ask her son about the princess's husband. But the Sun knew nothing about him and said the only hope of the princess was the Wind.

The mother of the Sun gave the princess a roast chicken to eat, and advised her to take great care of the bones. The second pair of shoes was worn through and the princess put on the last one. Then she took took her child and her staff and set forth on her way to the Wind.

In these wanderings she met with even greater difficulties than before, for she came upon mountains of flint, out of which tongues of fire would flare up; she passed through woods which had never been trodden by human feet, and had to cross fields of ice and avalanches of snow. Then she reached an enormous cave in the side of a mountain. This was where the Wind lived. The mother of the Wind took her in and fed her and gave her a bed to sleep in. In the morning she told her that her husband was living in a wild wood, so thick that no axe had been able to cut a way through it. She also gave her a chicken to eat and warned her to take care of the bones. Then she advised her to go by the Milky Way, which at night lies across the sky, and to wander on till she reached her goal.

Having thanked the mother of the Wind, the princess set out on her journey. She walked until her last pair of shoes fell in pieces. So she threw them away and went on with bare feet not heeding the thorns that wounded her, nor the stones that bruised her. At last she reached the wild wood and for three days and three nights she struggled through it. Her staff was no further help, for it had become blunted. Suddenly in the thicket she came upon a strange house. It had no windows and the door was up in the roof. How was she to get in?

She took the bones of the chickens out of her bundle and placed them together. To her surprise they stuck tight. So she made a ladder that reached the door in the roof of the house and that is how she could enter. Here she found everything in perfect order. Having taken some food, she laid the child down to sleep in a trough that was on the floor, and sat down herself to rest.

When her husband came back, for his house it was, he changed himself into a dove and flew to the roof and into the house. Here he found a woman rocking a child. At the sight of her, looking so changed by all that she had suffered for his sake, his heart was moved by such love and compassion, that he suddenly became a man. The princess embraced him and in her great joy forgot all the pain and misery she had endured. They sat down together and he told her his own history: "I am a king's son. I slew a dragon and his mother cast a spell over me and changed me into a pig. It was she who gave you the thread to bind my foot. But now that we have suffered for each other, and have found each other again, the spell is rescinded."

They went back to his kingdom, and great was the rejoicing of the people when they saw him and his wife. Then they set out to see her father. The old king nearly went out of his mind with joy at beholding his daughter again. He put them on the throne in his place, and they ruled as only those can rule who have suffered many things.

There are a good many versions of this particular fairytale in different languages, which means the message it wants to give to us is an important one. One of the best known versions is probably "East of the Sun, West of the Moon", where the enchanted animal bridegroom shapeshifting into a man at night is a bear instead of a pig. There is even a famous, rather exalted example of this interesting story written by Apuleius in Latin in the second century AD, the novel "Eros and Psyche" (in his "Metamorphoses", otherwise known as "The Golden Ass"). Here the pig part is taken on by the god of love, Eros. His mother, Aphrodite, is jealous of Psyche's great beauty and wants her to fall in love with a monster. Psyche is also (like the heroine in "The Enchanted Pig") the youngest of three princesses and, being sacrificed to said monster, who only visits her in the dead of night, she is very surprised and equally doomed when she finds out who the monster really is. If I had a choice between a pig, a bear and a god, I would go for the pig every day and twice on Sunday. Naturally the bear is also quite tempting. But a spoilt brat of a rather decadent Greek "god", no thank you. In the sacred dreamtime the very first gods and goddesses did quite frequently appear as animals. The great goddess delighted in shapeshifting into a pig, Anubis is a dog or a jackal, Hanuman a monkey, Ganesha an elephant and Hathor a cow. The word "Animal" (Anima) has in fact the same meaning as the word "Psyche": Soul!

In reality every animal IS a prince, and no arduous journey is needed to prove and confirm this. Still, Psyche's ordeal is worthwhile, because that is how she discovers her own divinity. Her story has inspired many artists, as early as the fourth century in Greece, and during the renaissance in Rome where Raphael painted her in the Villa Farnesia (Loggia di Psiche). Among the Pre-Raphaelites or English Dreamers Edward Burne Jones and John William Waterhouse were drawn to her.

So, what IS the message of all those interrelated stories? That we as human beings have far more responsibilities than we ever dreamed of. We all have to go the way of the princess, who married the pig, the bear or the wayward son of Aphrodite. We are no longer the children of a great king who can play in a beautiful sheltered paradise garden. We have to grow up. Nobody is going to save our planet and our souls if we do not do at least part of the job ourselves. So we had better get going!

The theme of the medicine wheel (the four directions) is vital in all versions of these fairytales. The medicine wheel is a symbol of earth. If we want to find our own divine selves we must first of all embrace the divine self of Gaia. So far we have learned to deal with East and West (emotions and mind) fairly well. But we tend to be stuck there because most of us fear the challenge of North and South (life and death). Here begins the final redemption and the ascension process of Gaia.

The famous Irish fairytale "The Children of Lir", in which the four children of the king (the four elements within the four directions) are transformed into swans and must swim in the wild Atlantic ocean until after many hundred years the king of the North marries the queen of the South, is one of the most beautiful metaphors of the ascension of our planet. The constrasts (North and South, life and death, light and shadow) disappear. All is one. All is light and love eternal.

The four kingdoms in ancient Ireland (Eire, Eriu) were spread out in the shape of a medicine wheel, with the high king in Tara in the middle. The origins of this were the four fairy kingdoms of the Tuatha De Danann, the shining ones, the immortals who now dwell in the hills, the hollow hills and in Tir Nan Og, the land of the ever young.

The enormous pig from the North that walks into the palace of the king of the South is the fulfilling of an ancient prophecy. On a table with a gorgeous cloth lies the wonderful book that tells the three princesses about his coming. That they simply have to open the forbidden room reminds us of the tree of knowledge in the garden of Eden.

Of course Eve and Adam wanted to eat the fruit of this. Who wouldn't? If we want to heal our planet and ourselves we must by necessity know the truth about all our illnesses. To forbid knowledge of any kind or the access to it is highly suspicious. It can only mean that the being who proclaims such a prohibition wants to control others and has its own secret agendas that are far from well meaning. The "god" of the old testament is such a very strange and at least halfway quite malevolent character. We don't need Carl Gustav Jung's interesting book "Answer to Job" to understand this fully. It is enough to read the bible really carefully and without religious blinders attached. A "god" who only cares for his "own people" and thus promotes war and racism is no god. A spirit who commands me to kill my child, a spirit who wants me to go to war and spare not even women and children and leave nothing but burned earth behind, is evil. A spirit who makes a bet with Satan and murders the firstborn of every family is not to be trusted. We are so gullible. If an entity tells us that he is the one and only god, we not only believe it, we even forget that we have a divine core ourselves. Our presently official religions (although rapidly dwindling) have bedevilled the gods of a past age. I hope our present gods will suffer the same destiny. The three leading monotheist religions of our time: judaism, christianity and islam, all suffer from the same illusion of grandeur: that they are the only right ones. Making all others first heretics, then enemies, then a declared danger and then a project for genocide. And all this of course by men, for men and about men. They're all that matters. These are truly men that made god in their own image: insecure, revengeful and dangerously wanton. The appeal of the three monotheistic religions at exclusivity has lead to more suffering, agony and deaths over the last three thousand years than any other cause. Us or them, we versus the others, friend or foe – trying to feel a bit elated by debasing all others.

There was a funeral in our village of a much beloved man. I heard a little girl of about five years of age ask her mother: "What happened to my uncle?" The mother said: "God has taken him." Whereupon the little one asked quite seriously: "Is god a monster?" The mother was dumbfound. I wasn't. I thought it was a very good question that deserved an honest answer.

As I said, we have to grow up, wake up and think for ourselves. There is no other way. It does not mean that we won't have a lot of help. As we can see even the mothers of the Moon and the Sun will give us shelter and advice and nourishment if we are willing to go the whole hog. And finally the wind becomes our ally.

What is a bit hard to envision in this fairytale is that the old witch Baba Yaga, the mother of dragons, and Aphrodite, the goddess of love, are really one and the same. We all know that we can find ourselves in every single character in every single fairytale, but that is not what I mean here. What I would like to point out is that in the final analysis good and evil are one, and if all is said and done, both must serve the divine plan and the sacred dream of creation.

The gigantic crime scene here on earth is not something we can simply escape through death or any other means. It will haunt us through lifetime after lifetime until we fully understand it and are ready to heal it. That is what the pig-prince means when he says his beloved will have to wear our three pairs of iron shoes and blunt a steel staff. The path of Psyche into the land of shadows is a mirror of Christ's path into the lower regions of the astral realm. It is well described too in the wandering of the pig-princess to the mountains of flints, out of which tongues of flame flare up, the woods that have never been trodden by human feet, the fields of ice and avalanches of snow, and finally the forest so thick no axe has been able to cut a way through it.

I remember a past life where I was a countess and the farmers around us had risen up in a rebellion that was crushed. The rebel farmers were hanged and I stood under the gallows feeling nothing at all. Then and there I was beginning to understand that those farmers and I were ONE. I was frozen with horror. But I knew. Christ on the cross was not only ONE with the sinners, he was touching the very heart of the mystery of all evil: endless separation. The significance of the big bang. The split up of one being into numberless galaxies, expanding and spreading out for ever into the void. At first this was simply fun and exhilaration and the ecstasy of creation. Pure conjecture and bliss. The ultimate freedom. But eventually something went horribly wrong. We fell from grace into what we now call threedimensional reality. Some of us managed to retain their spiritual nature and remain untouched by pain and death. The rest of us were not so lucky.

And now we have to find our way back into ONEness. We are multidimensional beings. Our origin is not human, we are children of eternal light undimmed by any shadow. The great Sufi poet Mewlana Jelalludin Rumi said: "Our death is our wedding with eternity. What is the secret? God is one." Could it not be that the true meaning of this is: God is ONEness?

The message of all those fairytales is not only important, it is urgent. We need to understand in wisdom, and in wisdom understand what the Greek mythology dimly surmised and the quantum physicists proved: that all creation is spirit. We need to understand this NOW! The mothers of the Sun and the Moon that harbour the pig-princess are spiritual concepts of Sun and Moon! The mother of the Wind is Sophia, the holy spirit, spiritus sanctus.

The emphasis on suffering in all those fairytales is a sore point with me. I VERY strongly object to every kind of sacrifice and to the glorification of martyrdom. When Christ was crucified he was an ascended master-being of light and he had learned to neutralize pain. We have no idea what his motivation really was or what he achieved through his actions. Anyway, to imitate his suffering seems rather pointless. Neither he nor Buddha wanted a politically organized religion. They both wanted all beings to be free. I firmly believe that Christ's give-away on the cross reclaimed the planet from dark forces and planted the seeds for its final healing and ascension. This is a very personal belief, and I have neither proof for it nor do I wish to push it on anyone.

As I have mentioned before, it is a sad pity that religion has a strong influence on lots of ancient fairytales, because religion often insists firmly on pain and death and sacrifice. Yes, I consider the path of the pig-princess to find her husband momentous. It is good to have an intent and to follow it through. But suffering does not make us better. If we are lucky it can teach us compassion, which we should use to be gentle to ourselves and others and to do our best to ease the pain of all beings on this planet and to promote joy and abundance, and certainly NOT to advertise suffering. The pig-prince is finally redeemed simply through his own love and compassion that he feels for his wife, and that he obviously did NOT feel for the dragon he killed or the dragon's mother.

Why are the chicken bones so very important? Without them the pig-princess could not enter her husbands house (and heart) and all her wanderings would have been for nothing. Maybe they are a symbol for the many gifts we daily receive from our earth mother and a reminder that we should treasure them. When the American Indians killed an animal they consulted their dreams before the hunt, they only chose a beast that was shown to them and they used every part of it. Nothing was wasted or thrown away.

Of course the tale of the pig-princess who walks throught the desert is also the story of the Shekina, who was sent into exile by patriarchs who basically feared and often hated women. The child she carries is the spirit child of a new golden age of peace and harmony.

The Green Knight

From Jutland

There lived once a king and a queen who had an only daughter, a charming and beautiful girl, dearer to them than anything else in the world. When the princess was twelve years old the queen fell sick, and nothing that could be done for her was of any use. As she was about to die, she sent for the king and said to him: "Promise me that whatever our daughter asks, you will do, no matter whether you wish to or not."

The king gave the promise and the queen died.

It happened that near the king's palace lived a noble lady whose little girl was the same age as the princess, and the two children were always together. The princess begged that this lady and her daughter should live with her in the palace. The king was not pleased for he distrusted the lady, but the princess wished so much for it that he did not like to refuse.

The lady and her daughter arrived and for a long time all went well. Then one day the lady came to the princess, dressed for a journey, saying: "Farewell, my child; my daughter and I must leave you and go far away."

The princess began to cry bitterly. "Oh! you must not leave me!" she sobbed, "Is there nothing that can keep you here?" – "Only one thing, and that is impossible." –

"Nothing is impossible. Tell me what it is, and it shall be done." – "If the king, your father, would make me his queen, I would stay."

The princess ran off to find her father, and begged him to marry the lady at once. The king turned quite pale. He did not like the countess, and so, of course, he did not wish to marry her. "I cannot do this, my child!" he said. But the princess cried so bitterly that, remembering his promise, he gave in and did marry the lady.

In a very short time the queen's manners towards the princess began to change. She was angry because she, instead of her own daughter, was heir to the throne. Instead of speaking kindly as before, her words became rough and cruel, and she even slapped the princess's face.

The king was very unhappy at seeing his daughter suffer. Calling her to him, he said: "You are no longer merry as you should be, and I fear that is the fault of your step-mother. I have built you a castle on the island in the lake, and that is to be your home. There you can do just as you like." The princess was delighted to hear this, and still more pleased when she saw the castle, which was full of beautiful things. For a long time she dwelt there in peace, and grew more and more beautiful every day. This was told to the queen, who hated her step-daughter still.

One day it was announced that a meeting of knights and nobles was to be held in a neighbouring kingdom. The king was amongst those invited. Before he set out he went to take leave of his daughter. She said to him: "You may greet the Green Knight from me." The king wondered at these words, for he had never heard of the Green Knight. When he came to the palace of the neighbouring king, the first thing he did was ask: "Can anyone tell me where I might find the Green Knight?" But nobody could.

When he started on his homeward journey he was sad because he could not do what the princess had wanted. He thought so much about it that he lost his way and presently found himself in the midst of a dense forest. He saw a man driving some pigs and asked him: "Can you tell me where I am?" – "You are in the Green Knight's forest", answered the man, "and these are his pigs."

Then the king rode on, he came to a second forest where about midday he reached a beautiful castle standing in the midst of the loveliest garden you can possibly imagine. On the edge of a marble basin sat a young man who was dressed in a suit of green armour. "This must be the Green Knight!" thought the king; and going up to him he said courteously: "I have come, sir, to give you my daughter's greeting." – "You are very welcome", replied the knight, "pray pass the night with me here."

As the sun was already set, the king was thankful to accept the invitation. Next morning, when he was about to set forth on his journey home, the Green Knight put into his hand a jewelled casket, saying: "Will your majesty graciously carry this gift to the princess, your daughter. It contains my portrait. I feel certain that she is the lady I have seen night after night in my dreams, and I must win her for my bride." The king gave the knight his blessing, and promised to take the gift to his daughter.

The princess was awaiting her father anxiously. "And did you see the Green Knight?" she asked. "Yes", answered the king, drawing out the casket, "and he begged me to give you this." When the princess saw the portrait she was delighted, and exclaimed: "It is indeed the man I have seen in my dreams! He and no other shall be my husband."

Very soon after the Green Knight arrived and when he recognized her as the lady he had so often dreamed of, he asked her to be his bride. The princess smiled and consented, but she said: "We must keep this a secret until the wedding-day, otherwise my step-mother will find a way to do us some evil."

For some time the Green Knight did visit the princess every day. But secrets are dangerous things, and sure enough the queen soon heard that the princess had a handsome suitor. She went down to the shore of the lake, where she hid herself behind a tree. She saw a knight, dressed in green leap into a boat and row over to the island. She remained by the lake all day until the knight returned. Then she took a poisoned nail and stuck it in the handle of the oar.

The next day the Green Knight went to visit the princess as usual; but as he took up the oar he felt a sharp scratch on his hand. It seemed such a little thing that he did not mention it to the princess. However when he reached home in the evening, he fell very ill and there was no one to attend him except his old nurse.

Of this the princess knew nothing. She waited day after day but the Green Knight did not return. Her father was travelling in a foreign country and she was all alone. One day, as she sat by the open window crying and feeling very sad, a little bird came und perched on a branch of a tree that stood just underneath.

"Tu-whit, tu-whit! Your beloved is sick!"
"Alas! What can I do?"
"Tu-whit, tu-whit! You must go to your father's palace!"
"And what shall I do there?"

"Tu-whit! There you will find a snake with nine young ones! Put them in a basket and go to the Green Knight's palace. Tu-whit! You must make a soup out of the snakes. Give it to the knight and he will be cured."

The princess went to her father's palace and looked for the snakes. She found the mother snake with nine little ones. She waited until the old snake left to sleep in the sun. Then she picked up the young ones, put them in a basket and ran off to find the Green Knights castle. All day she walked, sometimes stopping to pick wild berries or to drink from a brook. At last she came in sight of a castle, and just then she met a girl driving a flock of geese.

"Good day!" said the princess, "can you tell me if this is the castle of the Green Knight?" – "Yes, that it is", answered the goose-girl, "for I am driving his geese. But the Green Knight is very ill." – "Would you like to have a fine silk dress to wear?" – "Yes, that I would!" – "Then take off your dress and give it to me, and I will give you mine."

The girl could scarcely believe her ears, but the princess was already unfastening her beautiful dress and taking off her pretty red shoes. So the goose-girl lost no time in slipping out of her rough linen skirt and tunic. Then the princess put on the other's rags and went to the kitchen to ask for a place.

"Do you want a kitchen-maid?" she asked. "Yes, we do!" answered the cook who was too busy to ask the newcomer many questions.

The following day, after a good night's rest, the princess set about her new duties. The servants were speaking of their master and how very ill he was. The princess thought of the snakes and the bird's advice, and lifting her head from the pots and pans she was scouring, she said: "I know how to make a soup that has such a wonderful power that whoever tastes it is sure to be cured." At first they all laughed at her. But at last, when all the physicians had failed and the Green Knight lay dying, they decided that it would do no harm to try. The princess ran off joyfully to fetch her basket of snakes and make them into broth. She carried it to the knight, who took some and felt much better right away. The next day he had some more and on the third day he was perfectly well.

"Who are you?" he asked the girl, "was it you who made this soup that has cured me?" – "Yes!" answered the princess. "Choose then whatever you wish as a reward, and you shall have it." – "I would be your bride!" The Green Knight looked at her closely and knew her in spite of her dirty rags. You can think what a joyful meeting that was!

Soon after they were married in great splendour. The princess wore a dress that shone like the sun.

I have not yet found a fairytale where the king falls desperately ill and dies and the queen takes a new husband. It is usually the queen who must depart. Why? And why is the new mother usually so ill disposed towards her step-child?

The queens who die often represent the matriarchy that had to give way to patriarchy. In that case the new mother has to struggle for control, because women are now no longer in command, not even of their own person or their own children.

Why does the first queen utter such a strange wish on her death bed? We all know it is not good for children to have all their wishes fullfilled. They get utterly spoiled and they simply do not have enough experience to know the snares and dangers in life and have therefore not learned to avoid them.

Why would our children need parents or guardians if they were wise enough to do and to choose what is best? It is one of the responsibilities of grown-ups to set limits for the little ones and to keep them safe.

The promise the king makes now forces him to go against his instincts and to make not only himself but also his daughter unhappy. Why would his first wife have wanted this? Control games are a very tricky business. To want control after death is always fatal. In order to die well, we need to let go on a large scale. If possible before our last gasp. The sooner we learn to let be and set our loved ones free, the better! But now the dead queen rules through her daughter, as the king has to do anything she wants. A terrible state of affairs.

To live in our children may seem to be an interesting idea, but it is not possible, and if it were, it would certainly not be advisable. Our children have their own lives, and their very own thoughts and visions.

When the princess at last gets a slap in her face, I really think she richly deserves it for making her poor father marry a lady he dislikes and distrusts, and she would be all the better if she could learn something from this. Instead her Royal Highness is rewarded for her folly and gets her very own palace to do exactly as she pleases in it, while her father is stuck in his with the nasty wife.

There is instant karma and delayed karma. We are lucky if we reap the fruit of our deeds at once. But if we commit grave errors and nothing much happens, we are in trouble. When the heavy weather finally comes, you can bet that it will be very heavy indeed.

It is quite delightful that the Green Knight meets his future wife in his dreams! The princess too must be gifted in lucid dreaming for she sends her father to meet her bridegroom even though she has never met him before. Her castle in the lake sounds a bit like the habitat of the Lady of Shallot, who lived on an island entirely in her fantasies and gave them shape in marvellous tapestries until she beheld Sir Lancelot in her mirror and

She left her web, she left her loom,
She made three paces thro' the room,
She saw the water-lily bloom,
She saw the helmet and the plume,
She looked down to Camelot.
Out flew the web and floated wide;
The mirror crack'd from side to side;
"The curse is come upon me", cried
The Lady of Shallot.
(Alfred, Lord Tennyson)

For the Lady of Shallot the reality of the radiantly handsome, charismatic knight is too much for her. She takes a boat and travels in it to Camelot, but she dies before she gets there. But for the princess in our fairytale her dreams seem to come true and for a while she is happy with the Green Knight. Who is this Green Knight?

A character with this name appears in a 14th-century Arthurian poem "Sir Gawain and the Green Knight" and later in a fragmentary ballad "King Arthur and King Cornwall", where he is, besides Sir Lancelot, the most powerful knight in king Arthur's court. His skin and his clothes are green, the meaning of which has puzzled scholars very much. J.R.R. Tolkien called him "the most difficult character to interpret."

The Green Knight could be related to the Green Man of Celtic Mythology who appears in many old churches, a face surrounded by green and golden leaves, usually from an oak tree, and with leaves also coming out of his mouth. Other images are the Great Pan and of corse Dryads, tree spirits. In some fairytales the devil appears as a person dressed in green. One thing is certain: whoever he may be, he belongs to a past, long gone, when most of our planet was just one endless forest.

The Lady Greensleeves belongs to the same period as the Green Knight or the Green Man and is equally enigmatic. In our story no hint is given to us who the Green Knight could be. He appears in the princess's dreams, he woos her, he falls ill, and finally marries her. There is actually one small indication towards the Green Knight's origins: The king finds himself in a dense forest and has to pass through another forest before he can find his daughter's unknown bridegroom. The great Unknown. The very nature of the mystery that all those green characters share makes it clear that, like the angel in the crown of the tree of life, who is the mystery of divine light, the Green Knight, the Green Man and the Lady Greensleeves simply ARE the secret heart of the great forest.

To penetrate this mystery we might indeed have to marry it. But it is only too true that the forest has become dangerously ill. So, how can we heal our bridegroom? The princess listens to the little bird and then she goes to the stepmother who did the damage. This is a good plan, as it is likely she will have the antidote to the poison. In this case nine young snakes. The German word for "poison" is "Gift", this is quite appropriate because most poisonous plants are indeed gifts of healing. The snake too can produce poison and she is also a symbol of healing. The great healer Asklepios, who was the founder-father of the cradle of healing in Europe, the beautiful sanctuary in Epidauros, is always represented with a snake circling around his staff.

Why does the princess not simply appear as herself with her healing remedy? Why does she have to change clothes with the goose-girl? And why does the Green Knight not recognize her at once? He does not love her fine dress, but the woman inside it.

Once again we have to consider that in most fairytales time does not matter very much. Many lifetimes may be packed in one story. The spoiled princess, whose wishes are commands, must leave her castle, come down from her high horse and feel the earth under her feet. She must gather wild berries in the forest and become a goose girl and then a simple kitchen-maid. Only then she can understand the spirit of the forest and what is needed to heal it.

Only then can she truly love the Green Knight: the secret heart of the great forest. Only then is she ready to give herself to it and be one with it forever.

The Castle of Kerglas

From Brittany

Peronnik was a poor idiot who belonged to nobody, and he would have died of starvation if it had not been for the kindness of the village people, who gave him food whenever he chose to ask for it. And as for a bed, when night came, and he grew sleepy, he looked about for a heap of straw, and making a hole in it, crept in like a lizard. He was never unhappy and always thanked those who fed him, and sometimes would stop for a little and sing to them. He could imitate a lark so well that no one knew which was Peronnik and which was the bird.

He had been wandering in a forest one day, and when evening approached he felt very hungry. Luckily, just at that place the trees grew thinner, and he could see a small farmhouse a little way off. Peronnik went straight towards it, and he found the farmer's wife standing at the door, holding in her hands the large bowl out of which her children had eaten their supper.

"I am hungry, will you give me something to eat?" asked the boy. "If you can find anything in this bowl, you are welcome to it", answered she, and indeed there was not much left. But Peronnik ate what was there with a hearty appetite, and thought he had never tasted better food.

"It is made of the finest flour and mixed with the richest milk and stirred by the best cook in all the countryside!" he murmured, and though he said it to himself, the woman heard him.

"Poor innocent", she murmured, "I will cut him a slice of new bread!" And so she did. Peronnik was still eating it on the doorstep when an armed knight rode up.

"Can you tell me the way to the castle of Kerglas?" he asked.

"Are you really going to Kerglas?" cried the woman, turning pale.

"Yes, I have come from a country far off, and I am seeking the basin of gold and the lance of diamonds which are in the castle."

Peronnik looked up. "The basin and the lance are very precious", he said.

"More precious than all the crowns in the world", replied the stranger, "for not only will the basin of gold furnish you with the best food that you can dream of, but if you drink of it, it will cure you of any illness and will even bring the dead back to life. As to the diamond lance, that will cut through any stone and metal."

"And to whom do these wonders belong?" asked Peronnik in amazement.

"To a magician named Rogear who lives in the castle", answered the woman. "Every day he passes along here, mounted on a black mare, with a colt thirteen month old trotting behind him. But no one dares to attack him, as he always carries his lance."

"That is true", said the knight, "but there is a spell laid upon him which forbids him using it within the castle of Kerglas. The moment he enters, the basin and the lance are put away in a dark cellar, which no key but one can open. And that is the place where I wish to fight the magician."

"You will never overcome him, Sir Knight", replied the woman, shaking her head. "More than a hundred gentlemen have ridden past this house bent on the same errant, and not one has ever come back."

"I know that, good woman", returned the knight, "but then they did not have, like me, instructions from the hermit of Blavet." – "And what did the hermit tell you?" asked Peronnik. – "He told me that I should have to pass through a wood full of all sorts of enchantments and voices, which would try to frighten me and make me lose my way."

"Well, suppose you get through it safely?" asked the idiot.

"Then I shall meet a sort of dwarf armed with a sword of fire which burns to ashes all it touches. This dwarf guards an apple-tree, from which I must pluck an apple. Next I shall find the flower that laughs, protected by a lion.

I must pluck that flower and go on to the lake of dragons and fight the black man who holds in his hand the iron ball which never misses its mark and returns of its own accord to its master. After that, I enter the valley of pleasure. If I can find my way through this, I shall reach a river with only one ford, where a lady in black will be seated. She will mount my horse behind me, and tell me what I am to do next."

The woman shook her head and said: "You will never be able to do all that." The knight bade her to remember that these were only matters for men and galloped away.

The idiot wanted to go back into the forest but the woman asked him to tend her cattle, and he agreed.

One evening the boy was sitting alone on the edge of the forest, when a man with a white beard stopped beside him.

"Do you want to know the way to Kerglas?" asked the idiot, and the man answered: „I know it well, I am Rogear's elder brother, the wizard Bryak, and I always call his colt to guide me."

While Peronnik was herding the cows, he thought and thought how he could get hold of the black colt. One day he took a slice of bread and rubbed it with bacon fat and went out to the path down which Rogear always rode. He crumbled the bread on one side of it, and the colt smelt it and began greedily to lick up the pieces while the magician vanished round a corner. Peronnik threw a halter over his neck and leapt on his back. The colt turned into one of the wildest parts of the forest, while his rider sat trembling at the strange sights he saw. Sometimes the earth seemed to open in front of them and he was looking into a bottomless pit. He pulled down his knitted cap so as to cover his eyes, and trusted the colt to carry him down the right road.

At last the forest was left behind and they came to a shady park in which was standing a single apple-tree, its branches bowed down with the weight of its fruit. In front was the korigan, the little dwarf, holding in his hand the fiery sword. Peronnik told the korigan that he was the new servant engaged by Rogear, and since he was sitting on the back of the magician's colt, the dwarf believed him and he was even able to pluck one of the apples and ride on before the dwarf was able to stop him.

When they had left the park behind them, Peronnik and his steed found themselves in a narrow valley in which was a grove of trees, full of all sorts of sweet-smelling plants. Roses of every colour, lilies and honeysuckle, and above all towered a scarlet pansy whose face bore a strange expression. This was the flower that laughs, and no one who looked at it could help laughing too.

Peronnik gazed quite calmly at the lion guarding the flowers and removed his cap to show his respect. After wishing good fortune to the lion and his family, he once again announced that he was the new servant engaged by Rogear. He charmed the lion, as he had charmed the korigan, with his courtesy, and thanks to the mavellous speed of the black colt, he could gather the flower that laughs and escape the lion's teeth.

Now the path led to the lake of the dragons, which he had to swim across. The colt, which was accustomed to it, plunged into the water without hesitation and was soon on the other side of the lake.

The valley guarded by the black man now lay before him. He hid the colt behind a thicket of bushes and crawled along a ditch as close to the black man as he dared. The day was hot, Peronnik began to sing gently and kept going until the man was sound asleep.

On tiptoe the idiot crept back to the colt which he led over soft moss past the snoring black man and into the vale of pleasure. This was a delicious garden with fountains running with wine and tables spread with food, and lovely girls dancing on the grass calling him to join them.

Peronnik sniffed greedily the smell of the hot dishes and looked eagerly at the dancers. He almost stopped and he would have been lost, like others before him, when suddenly there came to him like a vision the golden bowl and the diamond lance. He ate some of the bread he had in his pocket and fixed his eyes steadily on the ears of the colt, and in this way he was able to reach the end of the garden, and at length perceived the castle of Kerglas, with the river between them which had only one ford. Would the lady be there, as the hermit of Blavet had foretold? Yes, surely that was she, sitting on a rock in a black dress, and her face the colour of a Moorish woman. Peronnik rode up and took off his cap more politely than ever, and asked if she did not wish to cross the river.

"I was waiting for you to help me do so!" she said as she jumped nimbly on the back of the colt.

"Do you know how to kill the evil magician?" asked the lady as they were crossing the ford.
"I thought that, being a magician, he was immortal", replied Peronnik.
"Persuade him to taste that apple, and he will die, and if that is not enough I will touch him with my finger, for I am the plague."
"And how am I to get the golden bowl and the diamond lance?"
"The flower that laughs opens all doors and lightens all darkness."

The evil sorcerer Rogear was sitting in front of his castle. As soon as he noticed the colt bearing Peronnik and the lady, he cried in a voice of thunder: "Why, it is surely the idiot, riding my colt thirteen months old."

"Great magician, you are right", answered Peronnik, "and I bring you two gifts. The apple of delight and the woman of submission."

"Well, give me the apple, and bid the woman to get down!" The idiot obeyed, but at the first taste of the apple the sorcerer staggered, and as the long finger of the lady touched him he fell down dead.

Peronnik entered the palace, bearing with him the flower that laughs. At length he reached a long flight of steps which seemed to lead into the bowels of the earth. Down he went till he came to a silver door without bar or key. Then he held up high the flower that laughs, and the door slowly swung back, displaying a deep cavern, which was as bright as the day from the shining of the golden bowl and the diamond lance. Peronnik took the bowl and the lance, and as he did so, the ground shook beneath him. The palace disappeared and the idiot found himself standing close to the forest where he had led the cattle to graze.

Peronnik made his way to the city of Nantes, which was besieged by the French. For miles around the country was bare, for the enemy had cut down every tree and burnt the corn. Inside the gate men were dying with famine. Peronnik drove away the French with his diamond lance, and the golden bowl restored all men and women and children to life.

No one knows what later became of the bowl and the lance. Some say it was once more stolen by an evil magician, and if you want to find them you must seek them as Peronnik did.

Peronnik is grateful to those who feed him and sings for them. The secret of happiness is to be thankful for all we have and appreciate it as a gift. Everything we have comes from the Lady Gaia, the Earth mother:

our clothes, our food, our drink, our houses and even our computers. It should be completely natural for us to share.

Idiots are children of light by nature. No wonder Peronnik can sing like a lark that flies high up into the blue sky.

The tale "The Castle of Kerglas" is a Breton version of the "Conte du Graal", the story of the holy grail, and of the evil magician Klingsor and the wounded Fisher King Amfortas. The quest of the holy grail was the greatest undertaking in the Arthurian legend. The grail is in some stories a precious stone (the philosopher's stone in alchemy), in others even a severed head (Peredur), and finally it is a cup with the blood of Christ, and at the bottom of that is the cauldron of Cerridwen. Cerridwen is a Welsh goddess and her cauldron of divine wisdom, rebirth and abundance was central to the religious mysteries of the past. Of course the cauldron is a symbol of the womb. The hugely popular stories of the holy grail are a nice try to take the privilege of giving birth (life) away from women and into the hands of men. But I feel strongly there is much more to the grail than this, and that is why I chose this fairytale.

In the castle of Kerglas the grail is a basin of gold that will give its owner the best food and a drink that can cure all illness and bring the dead back to life. Nectar and ambrosia, the food and drink of the immortals. The lance of diamonds relates to the bleeding lance that cut the body of Christ open when he was hanging on the cross. Its Celtic origin is the magic wand that was kept in the fairy kingdom of the South, it is a symbol of the sacred fire of creation. The magic wand is also symbolic for the lingham, the male sexual organ that can fertilize the egg in the womb (cauldron).

The wounded Fisher King (the disciple Peter was a fisherman) lives in a country that is a barren wasteland. Many knights from many lands have come to try to heal him and the land around him. Only Perceval succeeds. He is a fool like Peronnik. His story was first written by Chrétien de Troyes (1180, "Perceval, le Conte du Graal") and never finished, but his roots are deep in Celtic mythology. Britanny is, like Wales and Ireland, a Celtic country with a Celtic language.

For the American Indians the fool of the tribe, which they call the Heyoehkah, is of tremendous importance. He or she is related to the thunder bird, and if you have a calling to be a Heyoehkah and disregard it, you die. In the pueblo culture the Heyoehkah is identical with the Coyote, the trickster, in the Zuni culture with the Mud Heads.

For the Heyoehkah nothing is sacred. He or she dances outside all rules and laws of the tribe and can make fun of everything and everyone. But the Heyoehkah does not hurt anyone with his jokes because he has no ego agendas and serves the highest good unhampered by prejudices or traditions of any kind. In Ireland fairies can have Heyoehkah energy.

It is quite obvious that Peronnik is not at all stupid. His questions are intelligent, and he remembers what he hears. He does not use the basin of gold and the diamond lance for himself, he uses it to free and to heal his country.

It is quite obvious that the knight at the beginning of the fairytale does not reach his goal, even though he was taught by a hermit like Wolfram von Eschenbach's Parzifal. Maybe he is too arrogant and too sure of his success.

The quest of the holy grail is for men only. Since women are already in possession of a womb, this makes perfect sense. But why are the golden basin (grail) and the diamond lance in a dark cellar which no key but one can open? Magic and sexuality have both been thoroughly abused on our planet. We now have to deal worldwide with black magic, with pornography, prostitution, women trafficking and with the most horrible sexual crimes. The one and only key to white magic and to sacred sexuality is unconditional love, the flower that opens all doors, lightens all darkness and laughs so sweetly that everyone who beholds it laughs with it.

It is interesting that the seraph angel with the flaming sword guarding the garden of Eden becomes a korigan (dwarf) in our story. It certainly highlights the tremendous importance of dwarves in the spiritual realm. In "Snow White", they know all about the evil queen, her secret plans and calculations and she could never enter their house if Snow White did not invite her in despite all their warnings.

The apple tree that is guarded by the korigan is loaded with fruits. But they do not give eternal life or knowledge to the sorcerer Rogear, they kill him together with the plague. Black magic turns all things around, good becomes bad, and life becomes death.

Peronnik makes his way to the castle of Kerglas with a lovely mixture of innocence, cunning and courtesy. We often underrate courtesy. This is a shame, because it goes hand in hand with love. We should never take our nearest and dearest for granted or treat them without the respect every being deserves. And if we meet a stranger, the first order of the day is always kindness and good manners. I also greatly recommend courtesy of the heart in all relations with children, animals, plants and spirits. In honouring them, you honour yourself.

Like any storyteller before me, I changed some of the fairytales in this book according to my inner guidance. For instance, I don't see Peronnik as cruel. So I left out those bits and pieces that would make him appear so.

We now come to the black lady. In Chrétien de Troye's Perceval the high messenger of the Grail is a loathly lady (a repulsive crone). In Wolfram von Eschenbach's Parzifal (dated to the first quarter of the 13th century) she becomes "Condrie, la sorziere" and in Richard Wagner's opera the black lady is Kundry, at first a wild, unkempt, elderly woman, and later in Klingsor's garden a beautiful maiden and an evil temptress. Klingsor is Wagner's version of Rogear, a rejected knight who castrated himself. Klingsor's castle is the same as the castle of Kerglas, an evil sorcerer's lair. Parzifal withstands the temptation and pierces the veil of illusion by transforming his passion for a woman to compassion for earth itself. But Condrie or Kundry belongs actually to Montsalvatsch (Mons Salvationis), the castle of the holy grail. So what exactly does she do in Klingsor's realm? Wolfram von Eschenbach even introduces a second Condrie, a sister of the Arthurian knight Gawain, Condrie la Belle.

Men have a really hard time to make up their minds about the role of women around the grail. They compete with one another to make the main female as hideous as possible, and the winner is doubtless the plague, the black death. However, when a man at long last comes face to face with the grail, the girl who bears the golden cup is as radiant as the grail itself.

Carl Gustav Jung describes himself as Perceval in "The Red Book" and his wife, Emma, wrote a book about him. Like Chrétien de Troyes she died before she could complete it, and it was later finished by Marie-Louise von Franz. The two co-authors transform the doctrine of trinity into quaternity (father, son, holy spirit and Maria). In many Greek icons, the holy spirit IS Maria or Sophia. As we all know, the original trinity is the threefold goddess, maiden, mother and crone. In Emma Jung's book Maria is the grail. Marie-Louise von Franz said about the wounded fisher-king: "The wounded healer is the archetype of the self and at the bottom of all genuine healing procedures."

The black lady or the plague that rides with Peronnik is a particularly gruesome apparition of death, even worse than the grim reaper. It is rather difficult to recognise her as the high messenger of the grail, and yet without her, the idiot could not succeed. She knows the true nature of the flower that laughs, and she teaches it to Peronnik.

As I said, the quest of the grail is central to the stories around king Arthur and queen Ghwenhwywar. It is also an unavoidable task for each and every one of us. The search for the grail ends the brotherhood of the knights of Camelot. No more membership, not even of the highest order. The individuation processes have begun. Individuation means to be what you, and ONLY YOU, truly are. It is a lifelong task. The round table in Camelot suggests the idea of democracy: all are equal. If we enlarge that concept, the round table becomes the medicine wheel and the shamanistic practice of weaving together heaven and earth, which is the equality of animals, plants, humans and minerals.

In the first literary version of our fairytale (the story of Peredur) the grail is a severed head. The archaic ideal of kingship was the human sacrifice.

In an emergency the king had to be ready to die for his people and his land. The only historic fact concerning the life of king Arthur is his death after defending England for three days and nights against the brutal invaders from the North and from the South East.

Arthur never reaches the grail and his champion knight Lancelot only dreams of it. Gawain, whose power increases with the sun's rising and diminishes with its setting, comes close. Perceval at first fails miserably to heal the fisher-king and the barren land because he does not dare to trust his heart and his innermost feeling and knowing. But he gets a second chance and finally he becomes the grail's guardian. Only one knight becomes completely ONE with it and so ceases to be. Galahad.

A lightworker serves the light. Galahad IS light.

The universe cannot contain the grail and neither can our human form. The grail is all we ever wished for, and it also ends everything we desire. We have come into a realm where want is unknown. That does not mean we cannot still give a helping hand to those who need it, it only means that if we do so, we have a greater perspective than ever before.

The Three Wonderful Beggars

Serbia

There once lived a merchant whose name was Zlatan and whom people called "Zlatan the Rich." He was a very hard-hearted man, for he could not bear poor people, and if he caught sight of a beggar anywhere near his house, he would order the servants to drive him away, or would set the dogs on him.

One day three very poor old men came begging to the door, and just as he was going to let the fierce dogs loose on them, his little daughter Anastasia crept close to him and said: "Dear daddy, let the poor old men sleep here tonight, to please me!" Her father could not bear to refuse her, and the three beggars were allowed to sleep in a loft, and at night, when everyone in the house was fast asleep, little Anastasia, seeing a bright light, got up and climbed up to the loft, and peeped in. The three old men stood together, leaning on their sticks, with their long beards flowing down over their hands, and were talking together in low voices.

"What is the news?" asked the eldest.

"In the next village the peasant Ivan has just had his seventh son. What shall we name him, and what fortune shall we give him?" said the second. The third whispered: "Call him Vasilije, and give him all the property of the hard-hearted man in whose loft we stand, the one who wanted to drive us from his door."

In the morning Anastasia told her father what she had heard. Zlatan went to the next village and asked the priest about the children in his parish. "Yesterday", said the priest, "a boy was born in the poorest house in the village. I named him Vasilije. Who can be found to stand godfather to the little beggar boy?" The merchant's heart beat fast, and his mind was full of bad thoughts about the poor little baby. But he said he would be godfather himself and ordered a fine christening feast. After the ceremony Zlatan took the father of Vasilije aside and said: "Give the boy to me and I'll make something of him. I will give you a present of a thousand crowns. Is it a bargain?"

The father of Vasilije agreed. Zlatan counted out the money, wrapped the baby up in a fox skin, laid it in the sledge beside him and drove homewards. When he had driven some miles, he drew up, carried the child to the edge of a steep precipice and threw it over, muttering: "There now, try to take my property!"

Very soon after this some foreign merchants travelled along that same road on the way to see Zlatan and pay the twelve thousand crowns which they owed him. As they were passing near the precipice, they heard a sound of crying. Looking over the cliff they saw a little green meadow wedged in between two great heaps of snow, and on the meadow lay a baby amongst flowers.

The merchants picked up the child, wrapped it up carefully and drove on. When they saw Zlatan they told him about the child and showed it to him. Zlatan guessed at once that they had found his godson and said: "That is a nice little fellow. I should like to keep him. If you will make him over to me, I will let you off your debt."

The merchants were very pleased to make so good a bargain, left the child with Zlatan, and drove off. When they were gone, Zlatan put the child in a barrel and threw it into the sea. The barrel floated away into a great distance, and at last it floated close to a monastery. The monks were just spreading out their nets to dry on the shore, when they heard the sound of crying. It seemed to come from the barrel which was bobbing about near the water's edge. They drew it to the land and opened it, and there was a little child! When the abbot heard the news, he decided to bring up the boy, and named him Vasilije.

The boy lived with the monks and grew to be a gentle and handsome young man. No one could read, write or sing better than he, and as he did everything so well, the abbot made him wardrobe keeper. Now it happened about this time that the merchant Zlatan came to the monastery in the course of a journey. When he went into the church the choir was singing, and one voice was so clear and beautiful that he asked who it belonged to. Then the abbot told him the wonderful way in which Vasilije had come to them, and Zlatan saw clearly that this must be his godson whom he had twice tried to kill.

He said to the abbot: "I can't tell you how much I enjoy that young man's singing. If he could only come to me I would make him overseer of all my business. Do spare him to me. I will make his fortune, and will present the monastery with twenty thousand crowns." The abbot hesitated a good deal. He consulted all the other monks, and at last they decided that they ought not to stand in the way of Vasilije's good fortune.

Then Zlatan wrote a letter to his wife and gave it to Vasilije to take to her. In the letter he had written: "When the bearer of this arrives, take him into the soap factory, and when you pass near the great boiler, push him in. If you don't obey my orders I shall be very angry. This young man is a bad fellow who is sure to ruin us all if he lives."

Vasilije had a good voyage. On the way he met three beggars who asked him: "Where are you going, Vasilije?" - "I am going to the house of Zlatan the merchant and have a letter for his wife."

"Show us the letter."

Vasilije did as he was asked. They blew on the letter and gave it back to him, saying: "Now go and give the letter to Zlatan's wife. You will not be forsaken."

Vasilije reached the house and gave the letter. When the mistress read it, she could hardly believe her eyes and called for her daughter. In the letter was written, quite plainly: "Get ready for a wedding and let the bearer of this letter be married next day to my daughter." Anastasia looked at the young man, and he pleased her very much. So he was dressed in fine clothes and married to Anastasia.

In due time, Zlatan returned from his travels. His wife, daughter and son-in-law all went out to meet him. When Zlatan saw Vasilije, he flew into a terrible rage with his wife. "How dared you marry my daughter without my consent?" he cried. "I only carried out your orders", said she. "Here is your letter."

Zlatan read it. It was certainly his handwriting. He waited a month, and then he said to Vasilije: "I want you to go for me to my friend the Serpent King. Twelve years ago he built a castle on some land of mine. I want you to ask for the rent of those twelve years and also to find out from him what has become of my twelve ships which sailed away three years ago."

Vasilije dared not disobey. He said good-bye to his wife, who cried bitterly, and set out. As he tramped along he suddenly heard a voice saying: "Vasilije! Where are you going?" Vasilije looked about him and saw an old oak tree. He told the tree: "I am going to the Serpent King." – "When the time comes, remember me and ask the king: 'Rotten to the roots, half dead but still green, stands the old oak. Is it to stand much longer on earth?'"

Vasilije went on further. In time he came to a river and got into a waiting ferry boat. The old ferryman asked: "Are you going far, my friend?"

"I am going to the Serpent King."

"Then think of me and say to the king: 'For thirty years the ferryman has rowed to and fro. Will the tired old man have to row much longer?'"

Vasilije walked on. After a while he came to a narrow strait of the sea and across it lay a great whale over whose back the people walked as if it were a bridge. The whale said: "Do tell me where you are going!"

"I am going to the Serpent King!"

"Think of me and say to the king: 'The poor whale has been lying three years across the strait. Is he to lie there much longer?'"

"I will remember", said Vasilije. He walked and walked till he came to a splendid castle. The roof was covered with mother of pearl, which shone like a rainbow, and the sun glowed like fire on the crystal windows. Vasilije walked in and went from one room to another, astonished at all the precious things he saw. When he reached the last room, he found a beautiful girl sitting on a bed. As soon as she saw him, she said: "O Vasilije, what brings you to this accursed place?" He told her why he had come and all he had seen and heard on the way.

The girl said: "You have not been sent here to collect rents, but for your own destruction, so that the Serpent King may devour you." She had not time to say more, when the whole castle began to shake, and a rustling, hissing, groaning sound was heard. The girl quickly pushed Vasilije under the bed and whispered: "Listen to what the serpent and I will talk about!" The monster rushed into the room and threw itself panting on the bed, crying: "I have flown over half the world. I am tired and want to sleep. Scratch my head."

The beautiful girl sat down near to him, stroking his hideous head, and said in a sweet, coaxing voice: "You know everything in the world. After you left, I had such a wonderful dream. Will you tell me what it means?"

"Out with it then, quick! What was it?"

"An oak tree said to me: Rotten to the roots, half dead, and yet green stands the old oak. Is it to stand much longer on earth?" – "It must stand till someone comes and pushes it down. Then it will fall, and under its roots will be found more gold than even Zlatan the Rich has got."

Then I came to a river and the old ferryman said to me: "Will the tired old ferryman have to row much longer?" – "That depends on himself. If someone gets into the boat to be ferried across, the old man has only to push the boat off, and go his way without looking back. The man in the boat will then have to take his place."

"And at last I dreamt that I was walking over a bridge made of a whale's back, and the living bridge asked: 'Must I lie here much longer?'" – "He will have to lie there till he has thrown up the twelve ships which he has swallowed. Then he may plunge back into the sea and swim free."

And the Serpent King closed his eyes, turned round and began to snore so loud that the windows rattled. In haste the lovely girl helped Vasilije come out of his hiding place and showed him the way out. He thanked her with all his heart and hurried off.

When he reached the strait he told the whale how he could become free. The great fish heaved himself up and threw up the twelve ships. Then he shook himself for joy and plunged into the sea.

Soon after Vasilije reached the ferry, where the old man asked: "Did you think of me?" – "Yes indeed, and as soon as you have ferried me across I will tell you what you want to know." And he did.

At last Vasilije came to the old oak tree, gave it a good push, and over it fell. And behold, there at the roots was more gold than Zlatan the Rich had.

Now the twelve ships which the whale had thrown up came sailing along and anchored close by. On the deck of the first ship stood the three beggars whom Vasilije had met formerly, and they said: "Bless you, Vasilije!" Then they vanished, and he never saw them again.

The sailors carried all the gold from beneath the oak tree into the ships, and then they set sail for home with Vasilije on board.

Zlatan was more furious than ever. He had his horses harnessed and drove himself to the Serpent King. When he *reached the river he sprang into the ferryboat. The ferryman, however, did not get in but pushed the boat off.*

Vasilije led a good and happy life with his dear wife and his kind mother-in-law. He helped the poor and fed and clothed the hungry and naked, and all his children learned the value of compassion and mercy from an early age.

Zlatan is still ferrying people across the river. His face has become grey with old age, his hair and beard are as white, and his eyes have grown dim; but still he rows on.

"Zlatan" means "gold" in Serbian, and "Zlatan, the Rich" certainly has enough gold to be generous with beggars. But he obviously does not know that sharing creates abundance, and so he must loose his property.

The name of his little girl, Anastasia, means "Ascension". She helps the three beggars, and she also wants to help her father, but to no avail. Zlatan understands only one thing: money.

A very popular theme for icons are the three angels who visited Abraham to anounce the birth of his son. The most famous of these old testament trinity icons was painted by the Russian saint Andrei Rublev (1360–1430). Icons are not only considered to be sacred and fully alive, they can also perform miracles. An icon of Mary, the mother of Christ, once ended a war without spilling a drop of blood. The three wonderful beggars remind us of the three angels that represent the divine, and they certainly have miraculous powers.

Most Serbs are orthodox Christians, and the beautiful church of Saint Sava in Belgrad is one of the biggest orthodox churches in the entire world. Serbia was christianized during the reign of the emperor Heraclius (610–641) during the Byzantine papacy, and it has (after Bulgaria) the second oldest Slavic orthodox religion. Saint Sava (died 1236), the youngest son of the grand prince Stefan Nemanja, was the first archbishop of the autocephalous (self-headed, autonomous) Serbian church, the founder of Serbian law and literatur, and (like Saint Columban in Ireland and Scotland) a peacemaker and diplomat. Serbia has a rich cultural heritage.

Where does the story of Abraham and the three angels originate? It could be a legend that goes all the way back to the civilisation of Ur in Mesopotamia. Abraham came from the city state of Ur that dates back to about 3800 BC. It was once a coastal city near the mouth of the Euphrates on the Persian Gulf. The famous Ziggurat of Ur was a shrine to Nanna, the Sumerian Moon god. There are spiritual teachers who believe that the three wise men that came to the birth of Christ had come from Ur. However that might be, the three old men in our story are certainly wise. They know not only about the birth of a child miles away in the next village, they name it from afar and can decide his future. The name "Vasilije" comes from the Greek "Vasilios", meaning "king". The seventh child here in Ireland has often strong healing capacities. In numerology the number 7 is the seeker, the searcher of truth, and Vasilije, the seventh son of the peasant Ivan, is asked three times to find the truth on his pilgrimage to the Serpent King.

The three wonderful beggars are not content with wishing the little boy good fortune, they take further care of him. They make a green meadow and flowers appear in the snow, they guide the barrel to a monastery, where Vasilije can learn to read and write and sing, and finally they change his death sentence into a marriage feast.

Zlatan the Rich pays a lot of money to be given the opportunity to kill his godchild. The first bargain is made without consulting the mother of Vasilije. But then women barely exist in this fairytale anyway.

To be a godfather is a sacred task and not to be taken lightly. You stand in for the divine love and grace of higher powers. To abuse this great honour and privilege so blatantly is a very serious offence. When Zlatan finds out that Vasilije has been saved not only once or twice but three times from almost certain death, he could become aware that the young man is blessed and protected by something or someone greater than himself. Zlatan is given a chance to mend his ways while there is still time. But he is not only hard-hearted, he is also a very stupid and narrow-minded man.

The three beggars change the contents of the fateful letter. This is a motif that we find often in fairytales. They change it simply by breathing on it. Pneuma, the divine breath of creation. The letter contains death, the pneuma transforms death into life.

The second part of our story is almost identical to the German fairytale "Der Teufel mit den drei goldenen Haaren" (the Devil with the Three Golden Hairs). In the story of the Three Wonderful Beggars the Serpent King stands for the devil. Zlatan wants Vasilije to be destroyed but he only succeeds in making him more rich than he is himself. For some reason many fairytales give us the message that the devil knows everything. Of course the real wealth of Vasilije is not money but wisdom, which he gains through the monks who brought him up and, funny enough, by visiting the devil (Serpent King). As I said before, even evil must serve the light.

Have you ever "gone to the devil" or hit rock bottom? I have. Life is apt to throw those things at us. Did it make me wiser? Eventually, yes. Most of all, I was forced to discover the wonderful world within myself.

Just as a person who is paralysed or in prison can discover inner freedom.

It makes sense that the Serpent King is a friend of Zlatan and has built his castle on Zlatans land. They are one of a kind. Both are convinced that they own the planet and can do as they please.

But who is the beautiful girl residing with the Serpent King? The second part of our fairytale is crowded with metaphors. The oak tree, the ferryman, the whale and the girl.

Maybe the oak tree rotten at the roots, half dead and yet green is a metaphor for mankind. We could easily be pushed over and fall down, and once we do, all will be much better, because we can at long last start to regain our true divine nature. This is the gold beneath the roots of the old oak, and it is far more precious than any man's fortune.

The ferryman is an apt metaphor for a workaholic. If he stops at last, through death or otherwise, he will be replaced by another poor sod.

The whale who swallowed twelve ships is a metaphor for greed and avarice. The beautiful girl is the soul, the core-light. Every created being has a core-light, the devil as well as a saint.

Zlatan finally becomes a ferryman. Someone who rows to and fro seemingly for ever whether he wants to or not. All his life Zlatan cared more for money and business than for his soul or for his wife, his daughter or his servants. He is in a prison of his own making. He is not going anywhere. He is the rotten oaktree and the greedy whale rolled into one and he is the living proof that, when all is said and done, people cannot really harm anyone as much as themselves. Still, he too can be free. As the Serpent King said: It depends entirely on himself to push the boat off and go on his way without looking back. Maybe he became a merchant because his parents pushed him into it. Even as an old man he can still discover the secret of his own happiness and follow this road no matter what anyone else might think or say or do.

And what is the meaning of the twelve ships with the three wonderful beggars on deck? This is our spiritual heritage. It is all we have lost when we were captivated by matter and incarnated as "human beings" on this planet and forgot who we truly are.

I will end this book, as I started it, whispering to you and to myself: "Remember! Please remember! Remember the love, remember the light, remember the sacred dream of creation!"

About the artist and his paintings

Thomas Kay is a painter, sculptor and designer with a background in architecture. He was born and educated in Switzerland, then volunteered and travelled across Africa before settling in Ireland.

Together with Elisabeth Noel he founded the "Centre for Arts and Healing" in an old chapel at Bantry Bay.

Thomas Kay is moved and inspired by large stones engraved with enigmatic, abstract designs some four to five thousand years ago in the age of stone.

The artwork reproduced in this book are details of his series of paintings based on megalithic art (approx. 2500 BC) found in Ireland at Newgrange, Knowth, Fourknocks and Loughcrew in Co. Meath, Seefin in Co. Wicklow, Killin Hill in Co. Louth and Sess Kilgreen in Co. Tyrone.

In Ireland, megalithic art is almost exclusively found in connection with solar constructs - Newgrange being the most famous one - that are among the world's oldest remaining buildings. Often still intact and in working order, these impressive structures are a celebration of light, sacred geometry and the union of heaven and earth.

The visionary images and symbols carved in stone at these magical sites reveal the fundamental nature of ourselves, the earth and the universe. Like the themes of fairy tales, many of these motives recur around the globe.

Although accurately depicting the original carvings, often to scale - Thomas Kay takes liberties by overlaying complementary designs found on separate stones or even in different localities, by occasionally combining them with abstract shapes of his own, but mainly by recreating them in pure colour, silver and gold - to excite their radiant power.

The shape and size of the paintings reflect those of the engraved stones and therefore vary greatly - from A3 to one by three meters aproximately.

The various textures of the original paintings, ranging from dyed or raw hessian to reflecting metallic paint, allow them to change their appearance dramatically with changing light.

If you would like to find out more about Thomas Kay's work, the individual paintings or their background, please visit: www.kayartdesign.com

About the author

Elisabeth Noel was born in Switzerland. She has diplomas in Music and Drama and a wide experience in both.

Her spiritual background includes a three-year practitioner training in lightwork healing at the Dolphin Star Temple Mystery School (Mount Shasta, California), the study of the Kabbalah (Tree of Life) with the The Servants of the Light (a worldwide organization), and various shamanic studies at The Sacred Trust in England (Animal Spirit Medicine, The Way of the Melissae, Compassionate Depossession).

She is a musician, writer and works as a lightwork- and shamanic healing practitioner living in Ireland.

Elisabeth Noel offers workshops as a more personal way of sharing the wisdom and joy of fairy tales and lightwork. The venue is her lovely home and extensive forest garden on the sheepshead peninsula in West Cork. You can make shamanic journeys into the fairy realm (Tir nan Og), and you are invited to find and express your very own vision and interpretation regarding the ancient magic of fairy tales.

...come away, o human child, to the waters and the wild, with a fairy hand in hand... (W. B. Yeats)

For information contact: elisabeth.noel@starwater.ie

For other titles by Elisabeth Noel (in German language) see the following pages.

Jeder Mensch hat einen einzigartigen Zugang zum Königreich der Tiere. Eine solche Türe, die nur für einen bestimmten Menschen existiert, schliesst sich für immer bei seinem Tod, wenn es ihm nicht gelingt diese zufinden und zu öffnen – wie es Franz Kafka in seinem "Prozess" und in der Kurzgeschichte "Vor dem Gesetz" sehr eindringlich schildert.

DIE WEISSE KATZE zeigt nicht nur einen individuellen Zugang zur Tierwelt, es fordert uns auch auf unsere eigenen Grenzen zu überschreiten und zu begreifen, dass wir zwar eine menschliche Erfahrung machen, aber keineswegs in letzter Konsequenz Menschen sind oder sein müssen.

Tiermärchen aus verschiedenen Ländern der Erde helfen uns dabei uns selber und unsere treuesten Gefährten, die Tiere, neu zu entdecken. Wenn wir es wagen in die Abgründe der Schöpfung zu blicken und entscheidende Fragen zu stellen, zeigen sich ungeahnte Perspektiven zur Heilung und Ganzwerdung der Erde und all ihrer Bewohner.

ISBN 978-3-7322-4951-0

Märchen sind Goldadern der Weisheit, die rund um die Erde zu finden sind. Sie sind wie die Sterne am Himmel leuchtende Wegweiser der Traumzeit und führen uns unfehlbar zurück zu unserem göttlichen Ursprung.

Viele Märchen enthüllen uns auch unsere innige Verwandtschaft mit den Bäumen und mit der Pflanzenwelt. Die Bäume, die Blumen und Gräser sind aber nicht nur unsere Kinder, unsere Geschwister und unsere Vorfahren wie Aks und Embla (Esche und Ulme), sie sind auch unsere Verbindung zur Feenwelt und den Engeln und Devas, den Leuchtenden.

Wie bereits in ihrem Buch über die Tierwelt im Märchen versteht es Elisabeth Noel meisterhaft, die tiefer liegenden Weisheiten in den Mythen und Märchen der Menschheit herauszuarbeiten und ihre Bedeutung für Gesundheit und Heilung von Individuum und Gesellschaft aufzuzeigen.

ISBN 978-3-7347-5975-8